getting into

Business, Economics & Management Courses

James Burnett

8th Edition

Getting Into Business, Economics & Management Courses

This 8th edition published in 2009 by Trotman Publishing, an imprint of Crimson Publishing Limited, Westminster House, Kew Road, Richmond, Surrey TW9 2ND

© Trotman Publishing 2009   658.0071 Bur

Author James Burnett

7th edn by Kate Smith published in 2007
6th edn by Kate Smith published in 2005
5th edn by Fiona Hindle published in 2003
4th edn by Fiona Hindle published in 2001
3rd edn by Fiona Hindle published in 1999
2nd edn in 1996 as *Getting into Accountancy, Business Studies and Economics*
1st edn in 1994 as *Getting into Accountancy, Business Studies and Economics*

Editions 1–7 published by Trotman and Co Ltd

British Library Cataloguing in Publication Data
A catalogue record for this book is available from the British Library

ISBN 978 1 84455 187 3

Tables of UCAS tariff point systems under 'Further Information' (Chapter 9) reprinted with permission from UCAS.

Typeset by IDSUK (DataConnection) Ltd.
Printed and bound in the UK by Bell & Bain Ltd, Glasgow

Contents

About the author

James Burnett is a Director of Studies and careers and university advisor at Mander Portman Woodward. He has written a number of the Trotman/MPW guides including *Getting into Art & Design Courses* and he is a regular contributor to the education pages of the national newspapers and specialist careers publications.

Acknowledgements

I am indebted to Kate Smith, who wrote the previous version of this book, *Getting into Business & Management Courses*, and to Fiona Hindle, who wrote the original edition. I would like to thank Steve Cook, an education consultant, for his contributions to the economics sections, Victoria Yang, and also the many people who helped with earlier editions. This book would not have been possible without help from a number of university admissions tutors and I am grateful for their help. The views expressed in the book, unless otherwise attributed, are my own.

James Burnett

For up-to-date information on business, economics and management, go to www.mpw.co.uk/getintobus

Introduction

First and foremost, this guide aims to provide information and strategies for students interested in applying to study business studies, economics, management, or related courses at university. Although the book focuses on the three subjects in the title, the information and advice is equally applicable to applications for such courses as accounting and finance, banking, econometrics, or for joint honours courses such as mathematics and economics.

Throughout the book the examples that quote university entrance requirements use A level and AS level grades. However, the advice is applicable to students studying VCE and AVCE, Scottish Highers, the International Baccalaureate, and other qualifications. The UCAS website (www.ucas.com), in its 'Course Search' section, lists entrance requirements for all of the major examination systems. If you are unsure about what you need to achieve, the universities will be happy to give you advice. Contact details are given on all the university websites.

Following a career in business, economics or management is a very popular option for graduates, and students choose to do so for a variety of reasons. They gain the opportunity to develop their knowledge of management and domestic and international business through studying a range of theories, companies and organisations and by learning about and gaining practical experience of practical tasks such as business plans, negotiating and giving presentations. The courses are wide ranging and help students to develop a number of different professional, administrative, communication and technical skills to prepare them successfully for a future job in the field. Graduates with degrees in business, economics and management can go on to such diverse careers as advertising, banking and finance, insurance and teaching.

What do the terms 'business', 'economics' and 'management' actually mean and what do these jobs involve? If you are considering working in this field, this guide is designed to help you explore the entry routes and options available in higher education to start you on your career.

■ What do businesses do?

In its widest sense, a business is an organisation that exists to fulfil the purpose decided by its owners. This definition shows us just how varied and different businesses can be. Usually a business has to make a surplus on its trading (a profit) in order to be able to continue into the following year, but not all business owners see the profit motive as the single most important factor. Firms in leisure and tourism, the music industry or the media are all examples of businesses that are driven by the passions of those involved. Yes, some are also highly successful financially but it would be wrong to say that money was the sole driving force. Even those firms that might be regarded as more mainstream are increasingly aware of the image that they present to the general public and feel that this has to be taken into consideration alongside profits.

Businesses also vary greatly in the size of the company: some are vast public corporations, others small family-run concerns. Many of these multinationals are much larger than some countries. Of the top 100 entities in the world in terms of annual turnover, about half are multinationals and the other half are countries. Working for such large organisations will obviously feel completely different from working for small to medium-sized enterprises (SMEs) employing fewer than 250 people.

Whatever the size of the business, there are many differing approaches to the best way of running it. Business managers fulfil a variety of tasks and need a whole range of different skills. They need to inspire and give leadership, research, analyse and present information, think laterally in order to come up with imaginative answers, communicate with many different types of people, organise their own time and work to tight deadlines, design complex business strategies, solve conundrums, and trade off one interest against another. Jobs in business are never dull as the business world is constantly changing and firms are always up against their competitors on the one hand and changing consumer habits on the other. Even very big firms are not immune to failure and decline. The struggling high-street stores Marks & Spencer, WHSmith and Sainsbury's are a good illustration of this. However, these stores, amongst others, have seen a return to their past success recently, with an upturn in profits in 2006. Pressure on many high-street stores is now coming from online competitors.

The actual way a business is run in practice is referred to as the corporate culture. This includes all those many things that give the company its character. There are a number of different philosophies on best business practice and a variety of so-called business gurus who write books and run seminars on their ideas. Tom Peters, Peter Drucker and Charles Handy are some of the more famous gurus, but there are also more obscure approaches like the *Zen of Management* or *Pooh for Managers*. Cartoons like Dilbert point out just how often managers get it wrong and how frustrating this is for their subordinates.

■ What do economists do?

Economics is the study of goods, services and economies. Economics graduates find jobs in banking, insurance and tax as well as with governments and large organisations, such as the Bank of England. Some become academic or professional economists who develop economic theories; others manage money either for investment banks or governments. Some economics graduates follow careers in accountancy or management. Others work in the transport, manufacturing, communications, insurance and retail industries. Employers value students who have studied economics because they have well-developed analytical and critical thinking skills, and are good at problem solving. Economists learn to make decisions and come to conclusions based on analysis of numerical evidence: what are called **economic indicators**. Economic indicators include things like unemployment figures, exchange rates, share prices, inflation rates, and GDP. Economists use these indicators to assess whether markets or economies are likely to improve or worsen, and to then act accordingly. This could be on a small scale – whether it is sensible for a company to invest in building a new factory in another country, or on a much larger scale – should a government raise or lower interest rates to try to influence the inflation rate.

Economics can be split into two broad areas: **microeconomics** and **macroeconomics**. Microeconomics looks at the behaviour of markets and consumers. Examples of this include how businesses price their goods, and consumer spending habits (such as why they buy a more expensive brand of washing-up liquid when a cheaper one is available). Microeconomics looks at the small-scale decisions that affect our daily lives – if petrol prices rise, should you get rid of your car? Are higher wages an incentive to work harder or to work for fewer hours? It analyses different markets, from monopolies and oligopolies, to situations where there is proper competition between suppliers. Macroeconomics is the study of economies, and looks at issues that have an impact on a country's financial situation, for example inflation, balance of payments, exchange rates and the interrelationships between these. Macroeconomic issues are often the main headline on the news or in your newspaper – particularly at the moment!

01 Choosing your course

You should remember that a degree in business, economics or management is not always a prerequisite for a specific job, nor is it a guarantee of a high-flying job. However, these courses provide an excellent foundation and may give you a head start into the world of business or finance over other graduates. Some courses are biased towards particular areas – such as econometrics, marketing or personnel. If you already have an interest in a particular area, look for courses where this interest will be drawn out and developed.

You should also note that about 40% of vacancies advertised for graduates do not ask for a specific degree subject. Many potential employers are more interested in the class of a degree than its subject. If you do want to get into business but do not want to take business studies it should not matter that much – as long as you do well in what you do and end up with a minimum 2.i degree. But if you are set on studying business, economics or management at degree level, read on, because there are a huge number of courses available and you will need to do some serious planning.

What to consider

You are allowed five choices on the UCAS form. The basic factors to consider when choosing your degree course are:

- the kind of business, economics or management course you are looking for
- where you want to study
- your academic ability.

Going to university is an investment for your future and you need to squeeze the most out of your time there, so it pays to think hard about these points. They are all essential in helping you through the lengthy task of selecting what to study and where. From the huge number of institutions offering business, economics and management courses, it is advisable to start by narrowing down the options to between ten and 20. Once you have eliminated the bulk of the institutions and courses on offer, carry out your own detailed research.

- Contact your chosen universities or colleges and ask for their prospectuses (both official and alternative) and departmental brochures (if they exist) for more details. Remember that the universities' publications are promotional and may be selective about the information they provide.

■ Visit the websites of the universities you are considering. These websites often contain more up-to-date information than the prospectuses.

■ Attend university open days if you can, and talk to former or current students. Try to imagine if you would be happy living for three or four years in that environment and address issues such as whether you prefer to be on a campus or in a city and whether there are facilities for you to pursue your other interests and hobbies.

■ Talk to any people in business you know and ask for their views on the reputations of different universities and courses.

■ Find out what academic criteria they are looking for and be realistic about the grades you are expecting. Your teachers at school or college will be able to advise you on this.

■ Make sure the course allows you to select any particular options you are interested in by thoroughly checking out what is available. The list can sometimes be mind boggling! You will not always know what each option actually covers by its title, so read the department's own prospectus carefully and address any unanswered questions by contacting the admissions tutors direct.

■ Think about whether or not you would like a course that includes an industrial placement. This can give you extremely valuable experience and is a great opportunity to make useful contacts for the future. Employers also like graduates who have had a practical placement. It you do choose such a course, it is well worth your while checking whose responsibility it is to find you a placement. Does the university have a placement officer who will help you with this process, or is it entirely up to you to find something?

■ Do you want to spend some time abroad? If you are doing a course that has some foreign language content, it may be possible to do a work placement in that country. This could be particularly valuable as, not only would you gain practical work experience, but you would also improve your language skills, which could give you the edge when you come to look for a job after you graduate.

■ What are the computer and library facilities like at the university and the department you are applying to? If you do not have your own computer, how many terminals are available for the number of students that are likely to be using them? This can be very important when you are rushing to finish an important project report. You should also check on how readily available the books are that you require for the course. Remember, business and management books can be very expensive to buy.

■ Try to find out the reputation of the academic staff. If you are going to be taking a business and management degree you might prefer to be taught by academics who have some experience of business themselves. Use the internet to find out what their experience is and what they have published.

League tables

When you are trying to select your five university choices, you may find university league tables helpful, as they will give you an indication of how a university or a course is regarded. A word of warning – there are no official rankings of universities. The tables are normally compiled by the national newspapers and are based on a whole range of criteria. No two league tables will rank each university in the same way, nor will they produce the same results. However, they are a useful source of information and might be one of the factors you use to make your choices. The *Guardian* newspaper, in its 2008 tables (http://education.guardian.co.uk/universityguide2008/), ranked the top ten universities in the UK as shown below.

Table 1 Top Ten Universities – the *Guardian* 2008

1. Oxford
2. Cambridge
3. Imperial College
4. St Andrews
5. UCL
6. London School of Economics
7. Edinburgh
8. Warwick
9. Loughborough
10. Bath

Table 2 shows the *Guardian*'s 2008 rankings for economics courses.

Table 2 Top Ten Economics Courses – the *Guardian* 2008

1. Oxford
2. Cambridge
3. Warwick
4. London School of Economics
5. UCL
6. St Andrews
7. Birmingham
8. Edinburgh
9. Lancaster
10. Durham

Table 3 shows the *Guardian*'s 2008 rankings for business and management courses.

Table 3 Top Ten Business and Management Courses – the *Guardian* 2008

1. Oxford
2. Warwick
3. City
4. Bristol
5. London School of Economics
6. St Andrews
7. Bath
8. Lancaster
9. Strathclyde
10. Queen's, Belfast

But these rankings include a number of areas of assessment, some of which may not be relevant to you. The *Guardian*'s tables can be re-ordered on the website by clicking on a category that you think is most important. For example, we could look at the economics ranking, ordered by entrance grades of students being accepted onto the course (a good indication of the quality of the students).

Table 4 Top Ten Economics Courses Based on Entrance Grades – the *Guardian* 2008

1. Cambridge
2. Oxford
3. Edinburgh
4. London School of Economics
5. Nottingham
6. St Andrews
7. UCL
8. Warwick
9. York
10. Bath

We could also look, for example, at the ranking by job prospects, based on destinations of graduates.

Table 5 Top Ten University Rankings by Job Prospects – the *Guardian* 2008

1. Cambridge
2. London School of Economics
3. Warwick
4. Edinburgh
5. UCL
6. Aberdeen
7. Bristol
8. Durham
9. Leeds
10. Newcastle

Source: Education.Guardian.co.uk (Guardian News and Media Limited) http://education.guardian.co.uk/universityguide2008/

Once you have done this thorough research you should have a shortlist of universities that fulfil your criteria – the course that suits your needs, the location, and the ability to pursue your interests. From that you can choose the top five places to put down in the UCAS application.

Entrance examinations

If you are applying to Oxford or Cambridge universities you will have to sit an extra entrance examination. Details of these can be found in the MPW guide *Getting into Oxford and Cambridge*. Other universities will be introducing extra tests in the future, and you should check on the UCAS website or with the university to find out whether you will need to sit one of these tests.

Different courses available

What's in a name?

You are considering a career in a business- or financial-related field, and you want to find a suitable university course that will help you to achieve this. The university prospectuses that you sent off for have arrived, and so you settle down in a comfortable chair to read through them to make your choice of course. Two hours later, you are bewildered: should you choose business studies, business and management studies, management science, or business management? What is the difference between banking and finance, and international banking? Would a potential employer favour economics over econometrics? Why do some universities offer mathematics *with* economics whereas others only teach mathematics *and* economics? Hopefully, after reading this chapter, you will have a clearer idea about the course you should be considering.

Let us look at the courses listed on its website by that prestigious (but fictional!) institution, Melchester University.

- Accounting and Finance
- Banking and Finance
- Business Mathematics and Statistics
- Business and Management Studies
- Business Studies
- Econometrics and Mathematical Economics
- Economics
- Financial Economics
- Management (3 year)
- Management (4 year sandwich)
- Management Sciences
- Mathematics and Economics

The first thing to be aware of is that there is considerable overlap between many of these courses. As part of, for example, the business studies degree course, you would attend lectures on management – the same lectures that the management students attend. Additionally, in the second and third years of the course you will be offered options for the courses you wish to study, and so you would be able to steer your degree towards the areas that interest you most. This brings us to Rule Number 1 when choosing your courses:

Rule Number 1 – read through the course content for all three years. Do not just choose a course because of its title. You will find that the content of a particular course varies from university to university, and also that there is considerable choice available within a particular university's course. This is also important if you are interviewed (see Chapter 4) because you may well be asked to explain why you have chosen that course, and being able to discuss the course structure in detail will be an important factor in convincing the interviewer that you are a serious applicant.

Similar-sounding courses often have very different entrance require-ments in terms of both grade requirements and preferred A level sub-jects. A degree course in econometrics is likely to require a higher level of mathematical ability (possibly further mathematics to AS level or even A level) than economics, and some universities will differentiate between their *preferred* A level subjects (the more 'traditional' A levels such as mathematics, history, physics or economics) and *non-preferred* subjects (general studies, art, and media studies are examples of sub-jects that *some* universities do not like very much). Again, careful read-ing of the prospectus is important, because each university will have its own preferences or requirements.

The entrance requirement details for degree courses will always specify what examination results are necessary. These are either specified as grade requirements (for example, AAB) or tariff points (300 – see Chapter 9). When you apply through UCAS (unless you are applying post-results, that is, during your gap year), your teachers will put your predicted grades in your reference. You will need to find out in advance what they are going to predict, because this will affect your choice of universities and courses. There is no point in applying for five university courses that require ABB if your A level predictions are CCC. You will be rejected by all of your choices and you will then need to try to find alternatives through the UCAS Extra scheme, or through Clearing (see Chapter 6). Similarly, if you are predicted to achieve AAA, you are probably aiming too low if all of the courses you are applying for require DDD at A level. As a rough guide, if you are predicted, say, ABB, you might want to choose a course that requires AAB, three that require ABB, and one that demands BBB. This means that you have a good chance of getting a number of offers but it also gives you options if you do not quite meet the grade requirements when you get your results (see Chapter 6). So, Rules 2 and 3 are:

> ■ **Rule Number 2 – research the entrance requirements for each course and for each university, and choose the courses whose requirements mostly closely match your A level subjects and predicted grades.**
> ■ **Rule Number 3 – find out what your grade predictions are, and base your course choices on these.**

We will now look at some of the Melchester University courses in more detail. Bear in mind that courses with similar titles can differ significantly from university to university. These snapshots should be taken as an indication of what the courses involve. Your choices should be based on a thorough investigation of each university's course details, either in the prospectus or on the website.

Accounting and finance

Accounting and finance courses look at the financial aspects of companies and businesses. You will study accounting techniques, how companies assess their financial performance and how they plan for the future. It also covers aspects of management, share dealing and how companies are perceived by the public and by potential investors.

Courses you will take as part of the degree could include:

- elements of accounting and finance
- introduction to statistics
- managerial accounting
- principles of finance
- economic theories

- management science
- business mathematics
- commercial law.

Economics and econometrics

Economics is the study of income and expenditure, from small-scale situations (households, businesses) to global issues (how countries deal with income, spending, inflation, employment). It covers topics such as price-setting of goods, inflation, balance of payments and unemployment. Econometrics looks at how statistical methods are used to analyse and test economic theories.

Courses you will take as part of the degree could include:

- microeconomics
- macroeconomics
- mathematical methods
- statistics
- econometrics
- development economics
- accounting and finance
- game theory
- international economics
- labour economics.

Management

Management courses look at how organisations work effectively. The course will cover a broad range of topics, such as the structure of an organisation, financial management, and how people can be managed to get the best out of them. Management science is the study of how management methods are underpinned by analytical techniques and mathematical models.

Courses that you will take as part of your degree could include:

- economics
- psychology and behavioural science
- accounting and finance
- the process of management
- economics for management
- management science
- law.

Business studies

Business studies courses look at how businesses are run. A successful business model comprises a whole range of different issues, from marketing, advertising, location and markets, through to financial issues and management. It is a practical rather than theoretical subject, focusing on problem solving and real-life situations.

Courses that you will take as part of your degree could include:

- accounting
- organisational behaviour
- economics
- management science
- a market or business project
- international business
- marketing.

As you can see, there is a great deal of crossover of topics covered by these courses. A management degree will include some accounting, economics and business courses, and an economics degree will include aspects of accounting, management, finance and business. Business studies courses include modules on accounting, management and economics. The diagram below will give you an indication of the links between these courses, and the differences between them.

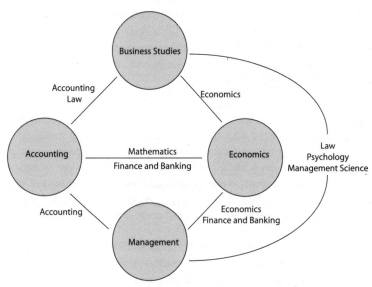

Degree courses showing common links between disciplines

Case study

'I didn't study Maths or Economics at A level and this made the first term a little harder for me than for other students on the course, but I quickly caught up. The thing that surprised me most was that economics requires a different approach from other subjects, because you have to think in a more abstract way, and to adapt and apply the economic models you are taught to real-life situations. There are formulaic ways to solve these problems – you have to approach them from many different angles, and to learn to try to comprehend the situations before trying to answer questions.'

Steve, former economics student at LSE

Single or joint honours?

If you are considering a single honours course, bear in mind that a good range of optional subjects might make it even more inviting. You may not want to be stuck with just a handful of choices from which to fill in your timetable after you have put down the core courses. Options may come from a similar field or a completely different discipline. Pinpointing specific subjects that you would like to study within your degree can help narrow your choice of university.

Most business and management courses include the core subjects of finance, economics, law, marketing, management and human resources.

In addition, most offer a range of options in the major areas of business such as marketing, finance, human resources, supply chain management, international business and trade, business strategy and small business management. Taking some relevant options may make you more attractive to a particular employer.

Alternatively, if you want to specialise in one other area, a joint honours degree might be more appealing. Some joint degrees do not require previous knowledge of the second subject. Others, especially those with a European language or a science-based discipline, often specify that candidates must have an A level, AS level or GCSE qualification, or equivalent, in a specific subject. In joint degrees, be wary of courses that have similar titles, such as business with German, and business and German. In the first, business is the major subject and German is the minor, but in the second, which is more likely to involve a year abroad, you will probably spend equal time on each subject. Economics and mathematical subjects go well together since economics is a theoretical subject, underpinned by mathematics and statistical methods. You will find a wide range of courses that combine economics with mathematics and/or statistics. For strong mathematicians, some of these courses may be easier to get offers for than the single honours economics courses. However, do not think that this is an easy way to get to study economics at a top university. These degrees will involve the study of mathematical topics to a high level, and so you need to be interested in mathematical subjects (and good at them) to get on to this type of course.

Exemptions

Are you thinking about going into accountancy, banking or insurance? Most commerce-related degrees contain modules that will give you exemptions from some of the examinations that aspiring professionals are obliged to sit for organisations such as the Chartered Institute of Marketing, the Chartered Institute of Personnel and Development and the various accountancy bodies. If you are concerned about which exemption subjects you can include within your degree, call the universities and ask which of the professional bodies recognise their courses. Alternatively, you can get in touch with individual professional bodies directly and they will tell you which university courses are officially accredited. Although taking exemptions as part of a degree course can be convenient, it is not disastrous for your career if you do not – but your professional qualifications may take around six extra months to complete.

Placements and overseas study

Studying abroad and/or completing a work placement could also be factors that affect your degree selection. It is possible to study business and management in dozens of countries across the globe as part of a degree based at a British university. Not all of these courses send you off for a full year though: there are schemes that only last for one term or semester. You do not need to be a linguist either as it is always possible to study overseas in an English-speaking location such as North America, South Africa, Australia or Malaysia. The availability of student exchanges has increased through programmes such as Erasmus, which encourage universities to provide international opportunities where practical – particularly in Europe. And the popularity of overseas study has encouraged some universities to develop special exchange relationships with universities further afield.

Methods of assessment and study

Degrees are usually assessed through a combination of examinations (normally spread over two or three years) and coursework, although individual units may be assessed purely by coursework or dissertation. Methods of studying, such as lectures, seminars, tutorials, practicals, workshops and self-study, tend not to vary much between universities (except for Oxford and Cambridge, where they centre around the one-to-one tutorial system). Some institutions, however, do offer part-time courses and even distance learning for a few of their degrees.

Location

While some students have a clear picture of where they want to study, others are fairly geographically mobile, preferring instead to concentrate on choosing the right degree course and see where they end up. But university life is not going to be solely about academic study. It is truly a growing experience – educationally, socially, culturally – and, besides, three or four years can really drag if you are not happy outside the lecture theatre. Below is an assortment of factors that might have some bearing on where you would like to study. See which ones you think are relevant to you and try to put them in order of importance. Again, the search facility on the UCAS website is a good starting point since you can begin your search by specifying regions within the UK where you would like to study.

Academic and career-related factors

Educational facilities

Is there a well-stocked and up-to-date business library nearby or will you have to fight other business and management students for the materials? Check for access to computer terminals if you do not have your own or may not have internet access in your room. If you are taking a joint degree involving sciences or languages, make sure there are facilities for your other subjects as well as science or language laboratories. The facilities available will depend on the budget of an institution and plentiful resources tend to attract better tutors.

Quality of teaching

This is difficult to establish without the benefit of an open day, but the Higher Education Funding Council for England, the Higher Education Funding Council for Wales, the Scottish Funding Council and the Department for Education and Learning of Northern Ireland have done the groundwork for you and assessed the level of teaching across the UK already. Their findings are publicly available – see www.hefce.ac.uk, www.hefcw.ac.uk, www.sfc.ac.uk and www.delni.gov.uk. Teaching quality may suffer if seminar or tutorial groups are too large, so try to compare group sizes for the same courses at different institutions.

Type of institution

There are basically three types of degree-awarding institutions: the 'old' universities, the 'new' universities and the colleges of higher education.

The 'old' universities

Traditionally the more academic universities, usually with higher admission requirements, the old universities are well established with good libraries and research facilities. They have a reputation for being resistant to change, but most have introduced modern elements into their degrees such as modular courses, an academic year split into two semesters and programmes like Erasmus.

The 'new' universities

Pre-1992 these were polytechnics, institutes or colleges. They form a separate group because they tend to still hold true to the original poly-technic mission of vocational courses and strong ties with industry, typi-cally through placements and work experience. Because of this there are a number of excellent business and management degree courses at new universities, which are very well regarded and highly competitive to get into. Some are still looked down upon by certain employers because of their generally lower academic entry requirements, but the new universi-ties have a good name for flexible admissions and learning, modern approaches to their degrees and good pastoral care.

Colleges of higher education

These are sometimes specialist institutions which provide excellent facilities in their chosen fields despite their size. They are sometimes affiliated to universities. This form of franchising means the college buys the right to teach the degree, which the university will award, provided that the course meets the standards set by the university.

Attractiveness to employers

Few employers will openly admit to giving preference to graduates from particular universities. Most are looking for high-quality degrees, often a 2.i or above, as an indication of strong academic ability. But since stu-dents with higher A level grades have tended to go to the old universi-ties, it is unsurprising that a large proportion of successful business people come from traditional university backgrounds.

A bit of research you can do yourself is to find out how past students have fared in the employment market. Ask to look at the university's annual final destinations survey, which should be available from the uni-versity's careers service, or the department itself.

Distance learning

The vast majority of students choose to study full time and complete their degrees in the shortest possible period. However, if you are a mature student or it would be more convenient to your circumstances, you might wish to explore the option of distance learning. According to the International Centre for Distance Learning there are approximately 15 business and business-related distance learning degree courses that you can study in the UK. Such courses include the BA in Business Studies at the University of East London, which states that 'students can take a shorter or longer time to complete the degree according to their needs and inclination'. However, students are normally expected to study one or two modules at any one time and take a minimum of three years to complete all 18 units.

The Open University also offers a BA degree course in Business Studies. There are no entry requirements for this degree, but the OU states that 'you must be suitably prepared for study at undergraduate level'. For further information, take a look at the website for the International Centre for Distance Learning at www-icdl.open.ac.uk.

Non-academic considerations

Finances

The cost of living is not the same across the UK, so will you be able to reach deeper into your pockets for rent or other fundamentals and entertainment if you are living in a big city or in the south?

Friends and family

Do you want to get away from them or stay as close as possible? While there can be advantages, financial at least, to living at home, you may prefer the challenge of looking after yourself and the opportunity to be completely independent. You may have deeply personal reasons for applying to a particular university, but it is not a good idea to go to an institution just because your best friend is studying there.

Accommodation

Do you want to live in halls of residence with other students, or in private housing that you may need to organise yourself and could be a considerable distance from college? Most institutions have an accommodation officer who will help you find a suitable place to live. And many universities will guarantee a room in halls of residence to first-year students anyway. But you will probably have to fend for yourself at some stage, so check on the availability of student housing, the cost and how far it is from the university. If your university is nearby, is there any point in moving out of home?

Entertainment

Are you going to be spending much time in, for example, the sports centre, the theatre or student bars? How about university societies – is there one that allows you to indulge your existing hobbies or caters for the ones you have always dreamt of trying?

Site and size

Many universities overcome the problems of urban v. rural and small v. large by locating their campuses on the edge of a major town (e.g. the University of Nottingham and the University of Kent) and centralising certain facilities and services to ensure safety, convenience and some sense of community, even on the largest and most widespread campus. But some students prefer to feel they are part of the local town or city community, rather than being isolated on an out-of-town site. Note that the bigger single-campus universities may cover a larger area than some of the smaller multi-site institutions. And do not be put off by the expression 'multi-site' – individual sites are likely to be self-contained so students do not have to travel to other sites too often.

Academic ability

For the majority of students, their A level scores will be the deciding criterion for selection. It is important to be realistic about the grades you are heading for: do not be too pessimistic, but do not kid yourself about your 'as yet undiscovered genius'. Talk to your teachers for an accurate picture of your predicted results. Some places specify particular grades but will still take you on if you get the same point score. So, for example, if you are supposed to get BBB (which amounts to 3 x 100 = 300 points), then any combination which produces 300 points (i.e. ABC or AAD) may be acceptable. However, you should not assume this.

Case study

'My path to reading business studies at university started at sixth-form college, where I was studying A levels in Biology, Economics and Politics. I enjoyed the independence I was given at college and the way I had to learn to become responsible for my own learning as I felt that this would stand me in good stead for university. Studying Economics at A level and having to read business-related articles in the newspapers and relevant magazines meant that I started gaining an interest in the more practical elements of business studies. I supplemented my interest with further reading and some work experience at a local telecommunications company. Although I did not have any responsibility at this stage, I shadowed a few members of staff, and observed many business practices. I then made the decision to study business studies at university and started researching my courses. It was hard to distinguish the courses that would best suit me from the huge number available but I looked at websites to find out exactly what the individual courses would entail and what options were available. I also thought very seriously about the location of the institution itself as I would have to live there for at least three years. I knew that I wanted to be in a town rather than the countryside, but did not want a big city. I was looking to really experience university life. I also wanted to ensure that the course would have a placement year so that I could get some hands-on business experience during my course.'

**Karolina, third-year business studies undergraduate,
City University**

Suggested timescale

YEAR 12

May/June: Do some serious thinking. Get ideas from friends, relatives, teachers, books, etc. If possible, visit some campuses before you go away anywhere during the summer.

June/July: Make a shortlist of your courses.

August: Lay your hands on copies of the official and alternative (student-written) prospectuses, and departmental brochures for extra detail. They can usually be found in school or college libraries, but all the information can also be found by looking at the university websites.

YEAR 13

September: Complete your application online and submit it to UCAS via a referee. It will be accepted from 1 September onwards.

15 October: Deadline for applying for places at Oxford or Cambridge.

November: Universities hold their open days and sometimes interviews. Entrance examinations for some Oxford and Cambridge courses.

15 January: Deadline for submitting your application to UCAS. (Late applications may be considered, but your chances are limited since some of the places will have already gone.)

April: Universities begin to make their decisions and offers will be sent directly to you.

15 May: You must tell UCAS which offer you have accepted firmly and which one is your backup. (The deadline is two weeks after the final decision you receive if this falls earlier.)

Spring: Fill out yet more forms – this time for fees and student loans, which you can get from your school, college or local authority.

Summer: Sit your exams and wait for the results. When the A level results are published, UCAS will get in touch and tell you whether your chosen universities have confirmed your conditional offers. Do not be too disappointed if you have not got in at your chosen institution: just get in touch with your school/college or careers office and wait until Clearing begins in mid-August when all remaining places are filled. You will be sent instructions on Clearing automatically, but it is up to you to get hold of the published lists of available places and to contact the universities directly.

For more details about UCAS and filling in your applications read *How to Complete Your UCAS Application.*

Case study

'Joint degrees are notorious for being hard work because you have two subjects to get to grips with, but I actually found that it suited me to have two subjects, because when I was fed up with one I could start studying the other for a break! In my third year I did a placement with one of the major accountancy firms. This allowed me to use my numeracy skills, but most importantly gave me a very good insight into business. I also spent some time in their management consultancy practice, which I thoroughly enjoyed. Working for a year was great. I felt like a real business person and coming back to university for my final year was really tough at first. However, I realised that I had to knuckle down to studying as I was in with a chance of getting a first. I concentrated and worked incredibly hard, and I was successful in getting my first class degree.'

Susannah, joint honours mathematics and business studies undergraduate, University of Surrey

---

Sources of finance

Studying is expensive. Unfortunately the reality of being a student is that you are likely to have incurred debt by the time you graduate. The latest figures show that average graduate debt is getting close to £15,000.

All UK and EU students pay tuition fees of up to £3,145 per year (2008 entry) as a contribution towards the cost of the course. Some students will have up to 100% of this paid by their local authority, depending on the income of their parents. Details of how these grants are calculated can be found on the Directgov website (www.direct.gov.uk). Even if you are not eligible for a grant, your fees may not have to be paid whilst you are studying – you can take out a loan for which repayments are not compulsory until you are working and earning more than £15,000 per year.

Scottish students who choose a Scottish university do not pay any tuition fees.

Welsh students studying in Wales will be charged up to £3,145 a year, but will receive a grant (non-repayable) of up to £1,890 per year to offset the fees.

The UCAS website (www.ucas.com) has full details of fees and support arrangements. The Student Loans Company's website is www.slc.co.uk

Some employers offer sponsorship to students on a vocational degree course such as business and management studies. It is worthwhile enquiring about the availability of any sponsorships by writing directly to personnel departments. Also get in touch with the university department and the careers service as they may have contacts with particular employers favourably disposed to sponsoring students. If you are successful, the deal is usually that you will work for the sponsoring organisation during the vacations. But this can give you excellent experience and, if you perform well, the prospect of a job offer after you graduate. If you are seeking sponsorship, contact employers as early as possible as it is common that applications need to be in well before the UCAS deadline.

02 Completing your UCAS application

The following advice should help you complete your UCAS application and, particularly, the personal statement. This is your opportunity to outline to the university admissions staff your reasons for wanting to study a business and management degree. More specific advice on filling in your application is given in *How to Complete Your UCAS Application*, updated annually (see booklist).

■ Competition for places

The competition for places at the higher ranked universities is intense and many candidates, whilst being successful at gaining a place on an economics or business-related degree course, do so either through Clearing or at one of their lower preference universities. Employers hold different courses and institutions in different levels of estimation. You should therefore do all that you can to ensure that your choice of university will stand you in good stead in the future.

There is particular competition for places on economics and management courses, with more applicants than places available. For example, for 2007 entry, UCAS reports that there were just over 7,000 applicants for about 5,700 economics places. At the top-ranked universities, there can be as many as 15–20 applicants for every place.

Because of the competition for places on highly ranked courses, it is particularly important to ensure that the personal statement section of your UCAS application is carefully constructed, and that your predicted grades are high enough so that your first choice universities are able to consider you. The personal statement of the UCAS application is the only chance you get to recommend yourself as a serious candidate worthy of a place. It is therefore vital that you think very carefully indeed about how to complete it so that it shows you in the best possible light. You must sell yourself to the department and make it hard for them not to take you.

Obviously, there are as many ways of completing your personal statement as there are candidates. There are no set rules, but some recommendations can be made.

The UCAS form

The UCAS form is completed online, via the UCAS website. There are five sections to complete:

- personal information – your name, address, nationality, how the course is going to be funded. This should be the easiest part of the form to complete, but you need to read the instructions carefully to avoid making mistakes.
- your choices of university. You are allowed to choose five courses. Again, pay particular attention to the course codes and university codes, and ensure that all the required information (where you intend to live, which campus you are applying to) is included.
- education – examination results, where you have studied, examinations to be sat.
- employment – if you have had gaps in your education because you were in employment, you need to give details here.
- personal statement – see below.

Once you have completed all of these sections, your referee will add his or her comments about your suitability for your chosen courses. This is normally done by someone at your school or college (such as a housemaster or head of sixth form) but for applicants who are not at school, this might be an employer (see Chapter 3).

The personal statement

The most important part of your UCAS application is the personal statement. This is where you have 47 lines to convince the five universities that you are applying to that:

- you are serious about wanting to study on the course
- you have researched the options available to you for the degree course and for your future career
- you are suitable for the course
- you are a well-rounded individual who can contribute to the life of the university.

Case study

'Economics is a subject based on analysis and mathematics. So I like it when students with a science background apply. I do not give preference to students who have Economics at A level over those that don't because I know that not all schools offer it. But I am very interested in students who have studied sciences, and I am less likely to offer places to students without at least AS Mathematics, unless they have studied a science. Apart from that, I like to see breadth in the A level choice. I will consider students who are studying one "non-preferred" subject (such as Art or Media Studies) but not in two out of the three A levels.'

An admissions tutor for economics

Before you start to write your personal statement, you need to finalise your choice of courses. Why? Because the personal statement has to convince an admissions tutor at a university that you are a serious applicant. It is important to remember that you write *one* personal statement that is read by the *five* universities. The people reading the personal statement do not know which other universities you are applying to, or for what courses. All they will be assessing is whether your personal statement is applicable for their particular course. If an admissions tutor is selecting students for an economics degree course, he or she will be looking for personal statements that address economics; if an admissions tutor is selecting students to study business studies, he or she will be expecting to read about business-related issues. It is important, therefore, to ensure that there is as much compatibility between your five choices as possible, otherwise you run the risk of being rejected by all of the universities.

Case study

'What am I looking for? Simple! Students who are interested in the study of management and the issues underpinning it, rather than those who simply want to be rich. Of course, ambition is important so I'm happy if they want to be rich *as well as* having a real interest in the subject. How do I assess whether they are interested in the subject? By what they have read and how they have investigated the subject – work experience is ideal. How do I know they have done these things? They write about them in the personal statement. Simple!'

An admissions tutor for management

The UCAS system allows applicants to apply for more than one course at a particular university. But beware: applying for two courses at the same university does not double your chances of studying there. As an example, take the case of a student who is desperate to study at Melchester. She decides to apply for both the economics and mathematics, and the single honours economics courses. What she is unaware of is that the Admissions Tutor for economics will look at her application for the two courses, *and* that the Admissions Tutor for mathematics will look at the application for the mathematics and economics course. Our applicant's main interest is economics, so her personal statement emphasises this, but it also devotes one paragraph to mathematics. The economics Admissions Tutor reading the personal statement will judge it on how it addresses economics, so he or she will either make offers for both courses or reject the student for both courses. The mathematics Admissions Tutor will be looking for evidence of an interest in mathematics, so he or she will probably reject the student for the mathematics and economics course because it is too focused on economics. By trying to increase her chances of getting to Melchester University, our applicant may in fact reduce her chances because her personal statement is neither focused enough on economics, nor is it specific enough about mathematics to satisfy the mathematics department at Melchester.

Rule Number 4 – when writing the personal statement, try to imagine how it will come across to each of the departments to which you are applying. Don't try to write something too general in order to allow yourself the luxury of applying to a wider range of courses.

The structure of the personal statement

There is no one formula for a perfect personal statement. It is called a *personal* statement because it should reflect your interests and achievements. However, as a general guideline, the personal statement should cover four general areas:

1| why you have chosen the course
2| how you have investigated whether the course is suitable for you
3| what makes you stand out from your peers
4| other information relevant to the application, for example if you are taking a gap year, what you will be doing during the year.

Why you have chosen the course
This could include:

- what first interested you in economics, business or management – for example, watching the news about the failure of a bank, an article in a newspaper about globalisation, or personal experience, e.g. work experience or the family business
- a particular career plan
- a combination of your particular interests and academic skills.

How you have investigated whether the course is suitable for you

- books, periodicals or websites that you read
- work experience (see Chapter 3)
- lectures that you have attended
- skills that you have gained from your A levels.

What makes you stand out from your peers

- academic achievements, for example, prizes or awards
- extracurricular activities and achievements

- responsibilities, for example school prefect, head of house, captain of netball
- voluntary or charity work
- evidence of teamwork, for example sports teams, Duke of Edinburgh expeditions, part-time jobs
- travel.

Other information relevant to the application

- gap year plans
- personal circumstances, for example it may be necessary for you to study in your home city because of the need to help to care for a disabled parent.

Case study

'My university probably has more applicants per place for economics than any other in the country, and it amuses me to hear the rumours that fly around amongst students about why we reject people. The most popular rumour is that we reject a student if they are applying to Oxford or Cambridge because we believe that they are not serious about us. What they don't understand is that I do not know where else they are applying to. I see my institution's name on the form, and the student's details and personal statement. However, I will reject someone if their personal statement does not address the issues that we ask them to write about – the information we require is made very clear on our website. So if a student has written a personal statement that is clearly aimed at another course, they may well be rejected.'

An admissions tutor for economics

A sample personal statement

I have chosen to study management at university because I want to run a business in the future, and management skills will be very important for this. I first became interested in management because my father runs a company and so I was able to see how important this aspect of the business is.

Last summer, I spent two weeks shadowing a department manager in a local company, and I gained an insight into the skills required to be a successful manager. In particular, I observed the need for good communication skills. I enjoy reading 'The Economist' and the business sections of the national newspapers.

I am studying Mathematics, Economics and Physics at A level. Mathematics is useful because it helps me to understand balance sheets and share prices which are essential skills for a successful business-man. Economics has taught me how a company's success depends on how it adapts to how the market is performing, and how it copes with fluctuations in the global economy. Physics teaches me how to be analytical and how to solve problems.

At school, I am captain of the 1st XV rugby team. This requires the ability to show leadership qualities and to manage people. It also allows me to get rid of stress. I play the trombone in the school orchestra, which involves teamwork and manual dexterity. I like reading, going to the cinema, and photography. I also have a passion for opera. On Saturdays, I work at the local Louisiana Fried Turkey fast-food restaurant, and so I have gained excellent communication and teamwork skills. In my gap year I hope to travel and to gain more work experience.

Points raised by this personal statement

- It is too short, less than 300 words. You should aim to use the full amount of space available.
- Although the candidate has addressed all of the relevant issues, there is a lack of detail. It is too general and tells us very little about the candidate.
- It is not very *personal*.

An admissions tutor's comments on the sample personal statement

Section 1: '*I have chosen to study management at university because I want to run a business in the future, and management skills will be very important for this*' (GIVE AN EXAMPLE OF WHY). '*I first became interested in management because my father runs a company*' (WHAT TYPE OF BUSINESS?) '*and so I was able to see how important this aspect of the business is.*' (AGAIN, GIVE AN EXAMPLE TO SHOW THAT YOU HAVE THOUGHT ABOUT THIS.)

Section 2: '*Last summer, I spent two weeks shadowing a department manager*' (WHICH DEPARTMENT?) '*in a local company,*' (GIVE DETAILS ABOUT THE COMPANY – WHAT DOES IT DO?) '*and I gained an insight into the skills required to be a successful manager. In particular, I observed the need for good communication skills.*' (GIVE AN EXAMPLE OF WHY THESE ARE IMPORTANT, SUCH AS DESCRIBING A SITUATION THAT YOU OBSERVED.) '*I enjoy reading "The Economist" and the business sections of the national newspapers.*' (GIVE AN EXAMPLE WHICH RELATES TO SOMETHING YOU HAVE STUDIED AT A LEVEL. THIS SHOULD BE THE STRONGEST,

AND LONGEST SECTION. I WANT TO KNOW MUCH MORE ABOUT WHAT THE APPLICANT GAINED FROM THE WORK EXPERIENCE AND WHY IT HAS CONVINCED HIM/HER THAT MY COURSE IS THE RIGHT ONE.)

Section 3: '*I am studying Mathematics, Economics and Physics at A level. Mathematics is useful because it helps me to understand balance sheets and share prices which are essential skills for a successful businessman. Economics has taught me how a company's success depends on how it adapts to how the market is performing, and how it copes with fluctuations in the global economy. Physics teaches me how to be analytical and how to solve problems.*' (THIS IS OK BUT COULD DO WITH LINKS BETWEEN WHAT THE APPLICANT HAS STUDIED AT A LEVEL, AND WHAT HE/SHE HAS DISCOVERED ABOUT BUSINESS AND MANAGEMENT IN THE REAL WORLD THROUGH READING AND WORK EXPERIENCE.)

Section 4: '*At school, I am captain of the 1st XV rugby team. This requires the ability to show leadership qualities and to manage people. It also allows me to get rid of stress. I play the trombone in the school orchestra, which involves teamwork and manual dexterity. I like reading, going to the cinema, and photography. I also have a passion for opera. On Saturdays, I work at the local Louisiana Fried Turkey fast-food restaurant, and so I have gained excellent communication and teamwork skills. In my gap year I hope to travel and to gain more work experience.*' (THIS SENTENCE COULD BE MORE DETAILED – RATHER THAN 'HOPE TO TRAVEL' I WOULD LIKE TO SEE SOMETHING MORE DEFINITE – 'I HAVE ARRANGED TO . . .' I WANT TO BE REASSURED THAT THE APPLICANT IS GOING TO USE THE GAP YEAR WISELY AND TO BENEFIT FROM IT.)

Adding the extra information requested by this admissions tutor would add detail, make it more interesting for him to read (so he is more likely to want to meet the student), demonstrate that the student is interested enough in the subject to be thinking about links between his studies and what he has experienced, and bring it up to the required length.

Rule Number 5 – Details turn an easily forgettable personal statement into something that will stand out from the others.

Your personal statement could include some of the following points:

My interest in the subject began because of:

- a newspaper article I read
- a book I read

- a news item
- my work experience
- my parents' work
- my A level subjects.

I have researched this subject by:

- reading books
- reading 'The Financial Times'
- reading 'The Economist'
- reading 'Business Week'
- work experience
- attending lectures
- talking to . . .

My work experience taught me:

- that the qualities a good manager/accountant/businessman/economist needs are . . .
- how to relate what I have been taught in A level Economics to real-life situations
- the importance of teamwork/accuracy/decision making . . .

Other relevant points:

- my A level subjects are useful because . . .
- my Saturday job is useful because . . .
- my role as school prefect has taught me . . .
- being captain of the 1st XV has taught me . . . (or netball, or leader of the orchestra, or . . .)
- during my gap year I have arranged to . . .
- I was awarded first prize for . . .

Work experience

Work experience is very useful as it demonstrates a commitment to the subject outside the classroom. Remember to include any experience, paid or voluntary. If you have had relevant work experience, mention it on your form. Explain concisely what your job entailed and what you got out of the whole experience. Even if you have not been able to get work experience, if you have spoken to anyone in business about their job it is worth mentioning as all this information builds up a picture of someone who is keen and has done some research. Wanting to be the next Richard Branson, Anita Roddick, Alan Sugar or Duncan Bannatyne are not good enough reasons to convince a hardened admissions tutor of your commitment to a business degree! You need to show them that you really do have some business and commercial awareness.

Although work experience that is directly related to the subject that you want to study at university (for example, work-shadowing in a bank if you are interested in economics) is extremely useful, remember that almost every imaginable job will be related in some way to business studies, management or economics. This applies to part-time work, such as a Saturday job as well as things you might do in your holidays. Helping in a local charity shop will give you insights into consumer behaviour and customer relations as much as a holiday job at the local supermarket. Working at Burger King once a week will teach you much about branding and marketing, corporate culture, quality control, economies of scale and customer relations.

General tips

- Keep a copy of your personal statement so you can remind yourself of all the wonderful things you said about yourself, should you be called for interview!
- Print off a copy of your application to remind yourself what you have said. Before submitting it, also ensure you check your application through very carefully for careless errors which are harder to see on screen.

The five rules for a successful application:

- **research the course content**
- **research the entry requirements**
- **find out your grade predictions**
- **ensure your personal statement focuses on the course**
- **include sufficient detail in the personal statement.**

---

03 Work experience and the gap year

Work experience

Getting work experience has become more and more significant in recent years, and in a climate where getting into business, economics and management is so fiercely competitive it is not enough to be only a brilliant academic. One of the things that an admissions tutor will look for is how serious you are about your chosen course (see the quote below). Many students decide to apply for a business- or finance-related course at university because they think it will be an easy route to becoming rich, rather than because they are actually interested in the course content and the skills that they will acquire from their studies. Work experience or work shadowing is an ideal way to demonstrate your commitment and show that you have done some research. If you can write about things that you saw or did on your work placement, and how they related to your A level studies, proposed university course, or future career, you will become a much more attractive proposition to the university selectors,

In addition, the more (ideally relevant) experience you have, the better the chance of succeeding in your initial job applications. Many employers will rate work experience as being almost as important as academic qualifications.

What will you gain from work experience?

- It will add weight to your personal statement.
- It will give you a true insight into the business or financial world and whether or not that is what you want to do. Some real experience will be particularly useful if you are trying to weigh up which area of business you would like to go into. For example, are you more analytical or creative? Would you be more suited to a career in finance or marketing?
- It helps you to make a better transition from education into the world of full-time work.
- It gives you the opportunity to build up those all-important contacts.
- It gives you a more impressive curriculum vitae (CV) – and will help you to gain excellent (hopefully!) references, which are important for any future career.

However, it is not that easy getting relevant work experience. Most employers recognise this and do not stipulate that it is essential, although it is preferred. If you cannot get experience in a large business, any work experience that demonstrates use of the skills employers are interested in will be valuable. Communication skills, determination, commercial awareness and IT skills can all be developed in many other sectors of business and commerce.

Case study

'What do I look for first in a personal statement? Work experience. Why? Because it shows that the student has thought about their future studies and done some research. It also makes for a much more interesting personal statement because they can write about what they observed and why it is relevant, so I am more likely to offer them a place. What students don't always appreciate is that my main jobs in the university are teaching and research. Being involved in admissions is an extra (albeit very enjoyable) burden. I tend to read the UCAS applications in the evenings after work, and might get through over a hundred in a night, and so the ones that make me interested in the applicant are more likely to go on the "offer" pile.'

An admissions tutor for economics

Looking for work experience

Marketing yourself

There is no single guaranteed way of succeeding in getting work experience, so try as many as you can think of, and be creative in the process. Here are a few suggestions.

- Ask your teachers at school/college if they have any contacts in the business world.
- Use your careers library and speak to your careers officer.
- Talk to your family and friends and ask them if they can suggest anyone to contact.
- Make sure everyone you know is aware you are looking for work experience.
- Send your CV and a covering letter to a variety of businesses local to you (see Chapter 3).
- Keep up to date by reading the business pages of the 'quality press'.
- Watch and listen to the business programmes on television and radio.

If you have a contact in a local organisation, try asking to go in for one or two weeks' work experience during the holidays, or even ask for one day's work shadowing to get an insight into what the working environment is like. Whichever route you take, it will almost certainly be on a voluntary basis unless you have specific skills to offer, such as good office and keyboard skills. If that is the case, you could try to get some paid work during the summer or register with an employment agency.

How to apply for work experience

It is never too early to start to put together a CV. This is a summary of what you have done in your life to date. If you have hardly any work experience, then one page on good quality A4 paper will be sufficient. If you are a mature student with a lot of jobs behind you there is some-times a case for going on to a second page, but for most young people a brief CV will be appropriate. Here are the main headings to cover:

Name; contact details; date of birth; nationality
These are the basic details to head your CV. Make sure they're right!

Education and qualifications
Start with your present course of study and work back to the beginning of secondary school. No primary schools please! List the qualifications with grades you already have and the ones you intend to sit.

Work experience
Start with the most recent. Do not worry if you have only had a Saturday job at the local shop or a paper round. Put it all down. Employers would rather see that you have done something, and every job will teach you some employment skills such as reliability, retail skills, etc.

Skills
List everything you do that could have a commercial application, such as computer skills, software packages used, typing, languages, driving licence, and so on.

Interests and positions of responsibility
What do you like to do in your spare time? If you hold or have held any positions of responsibility such as captain of a sports team, been a committee member or head boy or girl at school, put it all down. Do you play an instrument or have a creative hobby? Do you belong to a society or club? All these say something about the person you are.

Referees
Usually two: an academic referee, such as a teacher or head of your school, plus someone who knows you well personally, who is not a rela-tive, such as someone you have worked for.

Always highlight your good points on a CV and do not leave gaps. Always account for your time. If something such as illness prevented you from reaching your potential in your exams, point this out in your covering letter. To succeed in business you need to have excellent attention to detail, so make sure your spelling and grammar are perfect!

A sample CV

Lay out your CV clearly and logically, avoiding gaps and including any exams you are studying for as well as those taken. Below is an example.

Lucy Mathilda Johnson

Address 1 Melchester Road, Melchester MC2 3EF
Telephone 0123 456 7890   **Email** lmj@melchester.sch.uk
Date of birth 1 January 1989   **Nationality** British

Education 2000–2007: Melchester High School
2007: A levels to be taken: Geography, German, Mathematics
2006: AS level: Psychology (B)
2005: GCSEs: English (A), Mathematics (A), Geography (A), German (A), Biology (B), Chemistry (B), History (C), Physics (C)

Work Experience
2005–2007 (Saturdays)
Sales assistant in busy dry cleaner's in centre of York.
August 2006
Two weeks as temporary receptionist in small firm of accountants, responsible for answering telephone and general clerical work.
2003–2005 (Saturdays)
Delivering newspapers and magazines throughout my local area.

Skills
Modern languages – good written and spoken German.
IT – competent in MS Word and Excel, good keyboard skills.
Positions of Responsibility
Captain of school netball team, treasurer for Young Enterprise company.
Interests
Netball, swimming, reading, travel and music.
References
Available on request.

The covering letter

Every CV or application form should always be accompanied by a covering letter. The letter is important because it is usually the first thing a potential employer reads. Here are some tips on structuring and presenting your letter.

- The letter should be on the same A4 plain paper as your CV and it should look like a professional business document. Do not use lined paper and keep it to one side of A4 only.
- Try to find out the name of the person you should send your letter and CV to. It makes a great difference to the reader the more you can personalise your application – but do not be over familiar. Use their title (*Mr, Ms, Dr*, etc) and last name, not *'Dear Bob'*. (Get a book on business letter writing if you need help with the conventions. For example, if you start the letter *'Dear Mr Brown'* remember you should finish it *'Yours sincerely'*. If you do not know the recipient's name and send it, for example, to the personnel manager, begin with *'Dear Sir or Madam'* and finish with *'Yours faithfully'*.)
- The first paragraph should tell the reader why you are contacting them (e.g. 'I am writing to enquire whether you have any openings for work experience').
- The second paragraph should give them some information to make them interested in you by highlighting your interest in business along with some specific skills you can offer, such as knowledge of word processing or having a good telephone manner.
- Say in the letter if you know anything about the company and how you found out about it, for example if friends or family work there, or if you have read anything in the press recently that was of interest or relevant to your career prospects.
- Employers usually prefer typed letters, unless they specifically request one to be handwritten.

Whether you are applying for a position through an advertisement, or just sending a speculative letter to a local company, you should do plenty of research on the employer. Having some information will help you tailor your CV for that particular company, and it will certainly be impressive if at interview you show some knowledge of how the company works.

If you have an application form to fill in, follow the instructions carefully. Always complete forms neatly, using black ink. If your handwriting can be unclear, make sure that you take your time. You probably will not be asked to submit your CV as well, so always add evidence to the statements in your application forms.

It is imperative that you keep copies of all the letters, CVs and application forms you send off, not just so you can remember who you have applied to, but so that you have something to work from at an interview. You are bound to be asked to elaborate on things you have written about yourself, so do not say you have got a skill or an interest if you cannot back it up.

Taking a gap year

Most university admissions tutors are happy for students to take a gap year in between their final year at school or college and the start of their university courses. Of course, whether or not the gap year enhances or strengthens the application depends on what the gap year plans entail.

There are two application routes for students taking gap years. Students can either apply for *deferred entry*, that is, applying in the final year of the A level course for entry a year later. So, a student sitting A levels in June 2009 would apply for entry in September/October 2010, not 2009. Alternatively, students can apply at the start of the gap year, once the A level results are known.

There are advantages in both routes, depending on the student's plans and A level grades.

Deferred entry

- You will know where you are going to study in August, before you start your gap year.
- You will not need to interrupt your gap year plans for interviews.
- If you are unsuccessful in getting offers from your chosen universities or courses, you can reapply during the gap year.

Applying during the gap year

- You will know your examination grades and so you can target your application much more effectively.
- If your school is not predicting high grades, and you feel confident in achieving higher than the predictions, you do not run the risk of being rejected based on the predictions.

Whichever route you take, it is important to plan the gap year properly so that it is clear to the universities that you (and they) will benefit from it. The point of the gap year is to gain work or life experience, maturity and independence, or to earn money to help to fund your studies. Admissions tutors are not going to be impressed with a gap year that involves watching TV and sleeping, simply because you worked hard at your A levels and feel like a break from study.

Here is an excerpt from a personal statement:

> 'I am going to take a gap year during which I hope to travel and to gain more work experience.'

This is not going to convince the admissions tutors that a) you have actually made any plans at all, and b) this is a year that is likely to help you to develop or to bring new skills and ideas onto their courses.

A better version might be:

'During my gap year, I have arranged a placement with a local travel agent, where I will be assisting with planning group tours to various European countries. I hope that this will help me to understand more about how a company sets its prices and its budgets, particularly in a field where prices and exchange rates fluctuate on a day-to-day basis. The work experience will also be useful because from March I will be travelling in Asia, visiting India, Thailand, Vietnam and Cambodia. In Cambodia, I have arranged to teach English in an orphanage for one month. To fund this, I will be working in the evenings in a local restaurant whilst on my work placement with the travel company.'

This is much more impressive because the candidate has linked what she will do to her future degree course (business studies), and it is clear that she has thought carefully about what she will do during the year.

Students often use phrases such as '*I hope to . . .*' when '*I have arranged . . .*' or '*I have planned . . .*' are more likely to convince the university selectors that they are going to use the year usefully.

Gap year plans

Gap year plans do not have to involve travel to distant countries (although this is a useful and enjoyable thing to do). There are many fulfilling ways of using the gap year. The important thing is to be able to justify the plans either at the interview or in the personal statement. Other things you could consider include:

- internships
- full- or part-time employment to earn money or to gain experience
- full- or part-time courses, such as IT, art, languages or practical skills
- helping with a university research project
- voluntary or charity work
- community projects.

If you are not sure whether your chosen university will be happy for you to take a gap year, contact them at the start of your final year of A levels, and ask them. Many universities also include a statement of their gap year policies on their websites.

04 Succeeding at interview

Although many universities do not interview prospective students, there are still a number (including Oxford and Cambridge) that do, so if you are invited for an interview, here are some points to bear in mind.

- Remember that if you shine in your interview and impress the admissions staff, they may drop their grades slightly and make you a lower offer.
- Interviews need not be as daunting as you fear. Interviews are designed to help those asking the questions to find out as much about you as they can. It is important to make eye contact and show confident body language – and treat the experience positively as a chance to put yourself across well rather than as an obstacle course designed to catch you out.
- Interviewers are more interested in what you know than what you do not. If you are asked a question you do not know the answer to, say so. To waffle simply wastes time and lets you down. To lie, of course, is even worse, especially for anyone hoping to demonstrate integrity and honesty suited to a business career.
- Remember your future tutor might be among the people interviewing you. Enthusiasm and a strong commitment to your subject and above all, willingness to learn, are extremely important attitudes to convey.
- An ability to think on your feet is vital . . . another prerequisite for a career in business or management. Pre-learned answers never work. Putting forward an answer using examples and factual knowledge to reinforce your points will impress interviewers far more. Essential preparation includes revision of the personal statement section of your UCAS application, so do not include anything in your UCAS application that you are not prepared to speak about at interview.
- Questions may well be asked on your extracurricular activities. This is often a tactic designed to put you at your ease and to find out about the sort of person you are, therefore your answers should be thorough and enthusiastic.
- At the end of the interview, you will probably be asked if there is anything you would like to ask your interviewer. If there is nothing, then say that your interview has covered all that you had thought of. It is sensible, though, to have one or two questions of a serious kind – to do with the course, the tuition and so on – up your sleeve.

But it is not wise to ask anything that you could and should have found out from the prospectus.

■ Above all, end on a positive note and remember to smile! Make them remember you when they go through a list of 20 or more candidates at the end of the day.

Preparation for an interview

Preparation for an interview should be an intensification of the work you are already doing outside class for your A level courses. Interviewers will be looking for evidence of an academic interest and commitment that extends beyond the classroom. They will also be looking for an ability to apply the theories and methods that you have been learning in your A level courses to the real world.

Newspapers and magazines

As an A level student, you should already be reading a quality newspaper every weekday and at the weekends. Before your interview it is vital that you are aware of current affairs related to the course for which you are being interviewed. The *Financial Times* will give you a good grasp of business, as will reading the business sections of the other 'broadsheets'. You should also keep up to date with current affairs in general.

Magazines are another important source of comment on current issues and deeper analysis. *The Economist* is a popular example, but you may also find it helpful to pick up the more specialist magazines such as *Business Age*. Reading professionally written articles keeps you well informed of relevant current events and gives you the chance to see how professional writers use the vocabulary and language of business to communicate the news and their views. Magazines such as *Enterprise* and *Human Resources* may also have some articles of interest to you. You do not have to buy all these – visit libraries or use the web regularly to keep up to date with the business press.

Television and radio

It is also important to watch or listen to the news every day, again paying particular attention to business and economic news. Documentaries and programmes about the economy, business ventures, the politics of business and so on, can be enormously helpful in showing how what you are studying is applied to actual situations and events. *Panorama* is a good example of the sort of television programme it would be useful to watch. *The Apprentice* and *Dragon's Den* can also be very informative.

Radio 4 has its equivalent in *Money Box*, and the *Today* programme in the morning has up-to-the-minute reporting on economic and business developments, often with interviews given by those most closely involved.

It is a good idea to know the names of the chairman of the CBI and the governor of the Bank of England, for example, and the names of the country's top business people. You can make a point of listening to what they have to say when they appear on *Question Time* or *Newsnight* on television, or *Any Questions* on the radio.

This advice assumes that you will be taking a single honours business or management degree, but if you have chosen a joint or combined honours course, you will have to prepare yourself for questions on those subjects as well.

Essentially, the interview is a chance for you to demonstrate knowledge of, commitment to and enthusiasm for business. The only way to do this is to be extremely well informed. Interviewers will want to know your reasons for wishing to study business. It is important to be aware of the many aspects of business, e.g. marketing, finance, personnel – and be clear about the differences between the various functions.

Case study

'My first interview was a disaster. I had written about keeping up to date with current issues by reading *The Economist* and the second question they asked was about this week's edition. In fact, the last one I had read was three months before the interview. After that, they asked me about why I liked their course, and if it differed in content from others I had applied for. What they really wanted to know was had I read their prospectus. I hadn't, and I got rejected.'

Michael, on his interview for economics

The interview

Interview questions are likely to test your knowledge of business and economic events and developments in the real world. Any controversial related topics could well be brought up by interviewers and you should be well informed enough to have an opinion about them from a business point of view.

It is important that your answers are delivered in appropriate language. You will impress interviewers with fluent use of precise technical terms and thus detailed knowledge of the definitions of words and phrases used in business and economics is essential.

You might be asked which part of your A level courses you have most enjoyed. You need to think carefully about this before interview and, if possible, steer the interview in the direction of these topics so that you can display your knowledge.

Future plans and possible careers may also be discussed at interview. You will not be expected to have completely made up your mind about this but, by the same token, you will not be held to what you say at interview after you have left university. Previous work experience is useful and you should be able to recall the precise tasks you carried out during your employment and think about them before interview so that you can answer questions on them fully and well. Questions of this kind will be asked to see if you have an understanding of how business and management theories and methods are actually applied in the world outside school or college.

Interviewers will ask questions with a view to being in a position to form an opinion about the quality of your thought and your ability to negotiate. You may be presented with a real or supposed set of circumstances and then be asked to comment on their business implications.

Recent events are very likely to form a large part of the interview and are all possible as the basis for questions. An ability to see the opposite point of view while maintaining your own will mark you out as a strong business, economics and management degree candidate.

Do not forget that interview skills are greatly improved by practice. Chat through the issues we have discussed with your friends and then arrange for a careers officer, teacher or family friend to give you a mock interview.

In any interview situation it makes a better impression if you arrive in plenty of time for your interview and dress smartly and appropriately (people in business tend to look quite formal). Try to appear confident and enthusiastic in your interview – but listen carefully to the questions you are asked without interrupting and always answer honestly.

■ Work experience interviews

Most of the above-mentioned tips would equally apply if you are going for an interview for work experience. However, here are some additional tips.

- Think through why you want the job, and in particular why you want to work for that organisation.
- Research the employer thoroughly before interview. Look at their brochure and website.
- Plan in advance what you think your key selling points are to the employer and make sure you find an opportunity in the interview to get these across.
- Prepare a few questions to ask your interviewer at the end. You can demonstrate your preparation here by asking them about something you have read about the company recently, if appropriate.
- Remember a nice, firm, confident handshake at the beginning and end of the interview.

■ Possible interview questions

Questions may be straightforward and specific, but they can range to the vague and border on the seemingly irrelevant. Be prepared for more than the obvious, *'Why do you want to study management?'* But remember, you wouldn't have been invited for interview unless you were a serious candidate for a place on the course . . . so be confident and let your talents shine through.

Some of the following questions are obviously relevant either to academic or to work experience interviews but many could easily apply to both. Try practising your answers to these:

Question: *Why have you chosen to study management?*
Comment: Focus your answer to this question around how your studies and work experience have provided you with the motivation and interest to pursue this subject at university. This is an obvious starting point for your interviewers and they will probably want you to expand on the reasons for choosing your course that you highlighted in your personal statement. Assume that this question will arise and practise your answer to it: ensure that what you say is well structured and that you do not waffle – try to keep your answer relatively short and certainly no longer than two minutes.

Question: *Why do you want to study at this university?*
Comment: This is another standard opening question and one that you should certainly be prepared for. You could talk about why the location of the university appealed to you, or how you were attracted to it via a personal recommendation. A prime factor that distinguishes one institution from another is the course it offers. You will need to ensure that you have researched the course in some depth to see what is studied and how it is organised and structured.

Question: *Have you visited here before?*
Comment: If you have visited the university or attended an open day previously, this is your opportunity to mention it. Remember that the people conducting your interview will have contributed greatly to their department's open day and will welcome your feedback, but do keep it positive! Talk about it being a useful and informative occasion. Your interviewers will expect you to have done a lot of research into your chosen course and institution, so they will be expecting you to be well informed. (The university prospectuses and websites are good sources of information.) You do need to show that you are familiar with the particular institution that you are applying to. Answering this question by just saying, *'No, but all universities are pretty much the same'* will not improve your chances of getting a place.

Question: *What thoughts do you have on what you would like to do after you graduate?*

Comment: Of course you do not need to know exactly what career you would like to follow at the end of your degree at this stage – but you do need to have some thoughts on the kind of job you might be interested in. A possible answer might be: *'I would like a job that incorporates both my education and my practical skills: something combining my A level education with my working knowledge of customer service operations, entrepreneurial abilities and computer and administrative skills.'* If, on the other hand, you do have a clear idea about what you would like to go into in the future, then talk about this – but remember to justify your reasons.

Question: *How do you think you are doing with your A levels?*

Comment: The interviewer will know your predicted grades so you do not need to give too much information about these, but do state that you are working hard and making good progress. Talk about what topics you are studying at the moment, and if you are doing anything related to business and management. Elaborate on the aspects of the course you like, the skills you have gained and/or coursework projects where relevant. This is a relatively boring question, so take the opportunity to direct the conversation towards subjects that you are confident discussing and which will show you in the strongest light. Topics you would be happy talking about should be prepared in advance.

Question: *What has attracted you to this course in particular?*

Comment: This question, like the second one, enables you to show that you have thoroughly researched the particular course that you are applying for. You should draw on a particular aspect of the course that interests you and explain why. The university's website will generally give a precise breakdown of the core units that will be taught each year as well as the optional modules.

Question: *Tell me about any work experience you have had.*

Comment: This is an important question. Expand on the description of work experience that you gave in your personal statement. Do not just list the things you saw and did – mention how you felt about and reacted to what you were seeing and doing. Did you enjoy it? Was there anything that particularly interested or surprised you? Try to give as personal an account as possible.

Question: *What are the main things you learned from your work experience?*

Comment: This is another standard question which follows on naturally from the preceding one. Talk about the varied nature of your experience. There may have been things that surprised you about the functioning of a business or about new technology that was used. How did it differ from your expectations? You could try to link this with things that you have been taught at A level if you have studied business studies, economics or accounting. Work experience includes any part-time or weekend jobs that you might have done. The interviewer will understand that the main reason that you have your Saturday job in a clothes shop is to earn some extra money, but they will be interested in seeing if you have learned anything from the job that might be relevant to your future degree studies. There are many opportunities to do this. Take the example of the clothes shop: you could discuss:

- whether the shop is part of a nationwide chain, or whether it is an independent business – and the advantages and disadvantages of this
- how the shop advertises and markets its range of clothing
- who the target buyers are, and how the business targets them
- how the goods are priced, and who the main competitors are
- the managerial structure of the shop
- the effects of a recession or an economic boom (whichever is relevant at the time of your interview)
- where the clothes are made, and the implications of this for the UK's economy
- customer relations.

Question: *How do you keep up to date with current developments in economics?*
Comment: Economics (and business and management) issues change every day (see Chapter 8), and to demonstrate a genuine interest in these subjects requires you to keep up to date with current issues. You need to read quality newspapers on a daily basis, watch the news, and read specialist websites.

Question: *Have you followed any business cases in the news recently?*
Comment: As an A level student you should be reading a broadsheet newspaper every day. Talk about a recent article you have read and why you found it particularly interesting. This is another standard question that it is vital you prepare in advance. If you try to think of a topic off the top of your head without having given it any serious thought previously, you may find that you are out of your depth if you have to deal with further questions on the subject.

Question: *Have you spoken to any people in business about their work? Have you visited any businesses?*
Comment: Talk about people who work in business and about what they have told you, and why you have found what they said interesting or motivating. When discussing a business that you have visited, give a different example from the one that you talked about with reference to your work experience. Mention what you learned about the workings of this business and what you discovered about the way it operates.

■ Other possible questions

Below is a selection of questions that have been asked in university interviews. You can use these as a basis for a mock interview. Get someone who does not know you very well to ask you a selection of relevant questions from the list, and then get them to assess how convincing your answers are. If there are areas that are obviously in need of work, then you can do some research as preparation for the real interview. However, do not try to learn 'right' answers to all of these questions and then recite them parrot fashion at the interview. If you do this you will come across as having prepared your answers. There is also a danger that you will try to twist a question to suit one of your prepared answers, and you will appear to be trying to be evasive to the interviewer.

- *What areas of business are you interested in?*
- *How does economics affect your daily life?*
- *What makes a good businessperson or manager?*
- *Can you give me a quick summary of the underlying reasons for the credit crunch?*
- *Why do businesses fail?*
- *What is meant by 'marketing'?*
- *Why do share prices fluctuate?*
- *Is it a good thing that the Bank of England sets interest rates in the UK?*
- *What is microeconomics?*
- *What is macroeconomics?*
- *What is globalisation?*
- *Is globalisation a good thing?*
- *Who has responsibility for reducing global warming? Businesses or governments?*
- *Is the rapid growth of the economies of the BRIC countries a threat to the UK?*
- *I've got no questions but you have got five minutes to convince me you should have a place to study here.*
- *Tell me about a difficult situation in the past five years that you dealt with badly and explain how you could have handled it better.*
- *What achievements in the last five years are you most proud of?*
- *What are your strengths? Give some examples.*
- *What are your weaknesses? How do you plan to overcome them?*
- *Why do you want to study here?*
- *What do you know about our course?*
- *Why is the course suitable for you?*
- *What did you learn from your work experience?*
- *I see you have read X recently. Can you summarise the main arguments?*
- *What have you read in the news recently that has interested you?*

05 Non-standard applications

Not all students who apply for degree courses are studying A levels or their equivalent. The term 'non-standard' could be applied to many different scenarios. Perhaps you are studying for a mixture of examination qualifications, or you have had a gap in your education. You may have already started a degree course in another discipline and want to change direction. Whatever your situation, the first thing you should do is make contact with some universities (either by telephone, or via the email addresses given on the university websites) to explain your situation and ask for advice.

We will look at two of the more common types of non-standard application in more detail: mature students and international students who are applying from their own countries make up a small, but significant, proportion of those applying for business, economics and management courses.

Mature students

Mature students fall into three categories:

- those with appropriate qualifications, for example, A levels, but who did not go to university and are now applying after a gap of a few years
- those applying for a second degree, having graduated in a different discipline
- those who have no A levels or equivalent qualifications.

If you are in the first two of these categories you can apply using the same route as first-time applicants. However, it is worth contacting universities directly to discuss your situation with them, and to get their advice.

A levels need not be the only entry pathway. Many universities now encourage mature students (who may have missed out on the opportunity to enter higher education immediately after school) to apply for entry to degree courses, taking into account their work experience and commitment as part of the entry criteria. There are now Access courses in colleges around the country that specifically prepare mature students for higher education. Mature students make up a growing percentage of the intake of university departments, often coming to their degree studies with valuable relevant experience of the workplace. Your local careers office or library will have details of these. It is also worth contacting universities to see which courses they recognise or recommend.

The main difficulty for mature higher education entrants is that they may not be as accustomed to study as the 18- or 19-year-old entrant. However, they possess an advantage in that they have experienced some of the everyday practical problems they will face in their future careers, and they therefore bring important work skills to their studies. Again, it is worth contacting universities for their advice. As well as being able to give you advice about your eligibility for the course, they will be able to give you details of the Access courses that they recognise. Mature students apply using the same application process as school-leavers: the online UCAS 'Apply' system. But whereas a student who is at school or college (or who is taking a gap year) will say 'yes' to the question *'Are you applying through a school or college'* (and will then be asked for a 'buzzword' – a password that identifies their school or college), mature students will submit the form independently. The main difference is that when the school/college student completes the form, it will be forwarded to the person writing the reference, who will in turn send it to UCAS, whereas the mature student will add the reference directly to the form. This means that he or she needs to make arrangements for someone to write the reference and have it available to paste into the form. Who is going to be a suitable referee depends on the applicant's situation: it could be a current or recent employer, someone who once taught the student, or someone who knows the applicant well. If you are in this situation, make sure that your referee reads the information on the UCAS website about how to write a reference, in order to ensure that it contains the information that the selectors are looking for.

The other main difference will be in the 'Employment' section of the form. This should be as detailed as possible and any gaps, for instance if the applicant has been travelling, should be explained either in the personal statement or by the referee.

■ International students

International students fall into three categories:

- those who are following A level (or equivalent) programmes either in the UK or in their home countries
- those who are studying for local qualifications that are recognised as being equivalent to A levels, in their own countries
- those whose current academic programmes are not equivalent to A levels.

Students in the first category will apply through UCAS in the normal way. All of the information in this book is equally applicable to them.

However, non-EU students will pay higher fees than UK or EU students. Whereas UK and EU students will pay around £3,000 a year for their degree courses (see Chapter 1), students from outside of these regions will pay anything from £10,000 to £16,000 a year for tuition. Accommodation and meals will be extra. How much living costs are depends on where you study, but as a rough guide, about £800 a month should cover food, accommodation, books and some entertainment costs.

Students studying qualifications that are accepted in place of A levels can also apply through UCAS in the normal way, from their own countries. The UCAS website (www.ucas.com) contains information on the equivalence of non-UK qualifications. These include the Irish Leaving Certificate and the European Baccalaureate. Information on the equivalence of other qualifications can be found on the UK government's qualifications website (www.naric.org.uk).

Students who do not have UK-recognised qualifications will need to follow a pre-university course before applying for the degree course. These include:

- university Foundation courses at UK colleges and universities. These normally last one year
- university Foundation courses set up by, or approved by UK universities or colleges, but taught in the students' home countries
- A level courses (normally two years, but in some cases this can be condensed into one year) in schools and colleges in the UK.

A levels allow students to apply to any of the UK universities, including the top-ranked universities such as Oxford, Cambridge and London School of Economics. Foundation courses are not recognised by all UK universities. You should check with your preferred universities about which courses they accept before committing yourself. Representatives of UK universities, schools and colleges regularly visit many countries around the world to promote their institutions and to give advice. You can also contact the British Council to get help with your application.

What happens next

Replies from the universities

After your application has been assessed by the university, you will receive a response. You can also follow the progress of your application using the online Track facility on the UCAS website. You will receive one of three possible responses from each university:

- conditional offer
- unconditional offer
- rejection.

If you receive a conditional offer, you will be told what you need to achieve in your A levels. This could be in grade terms, for example AAB (and the university might specify a particular grade in a particular subject – AAB, with an A in Economics), or in UCAS tariff points (300 points from three A levels – see Chapter 9). Unconditional Offers can be given to students who have already sat their A levels, such as gap year students applying post-results. Rejection means that you have been unsuccessful in your application to that university.

If you receive five rejections, then you can enter the UCAS Extra scheme, through which you can make additional choices.

Once you have received responses from all five universities, you will need to make your choice of the university offer you wish to accept. This is called your *firm choice*. You can also choose an *insurance* offer, effectively a second choice with a lower grade requirement. UCAS will give you a deadline of about a month from the date that you received your fifth response.

Results day

The A level results will arrive at your school on the third Thursday in August. Scottish Higher results come out in early August, and IB results are issued in July. The universities will have received the A level and Scottish Higher results a few days earlier. You must make sure that you are at home on the day the results are published. Don't wait for the school to post the results slip to you. Get the staff to tell you the news as soon as possible. If you need to act to secure a place, you may have to act quickly. This chapter will take you through the steps you should follow – for example you may need to use the Clearing system because you have not achieved the grades that you needed. Results from other examination systems are not automatically sent to UCAS or to the universities, so you may need to fax or email these to the universities when you receive them.

What to do if things go wrong during the exams

If something happens when you are preparing for or actually taking the exams which prevents you from doing your best, you must notify both the exam board and the universities that have made you offers. This notification will come best from your head teacher and should include your UCAS number. Send it off at once: it is no good waiting for disappointing results and then telling everyone that you were ill at the time but said nothing to anyone. Exam boards can give you special consideration if the appropriate forms are sent to them by the school, along with supporting evidence.

Your extenuating circumstances must be convincing. A 'slight sore throat' won't do! If you really are sufficiently ill to be unable to prepare for the exams or to perform effectively during them, you must consult your GP and obtain a letter describing your condition.

The other main cause of under-performance is distressing events at home. If a member of your immediate family is very seriously ill, you should explain this to your head teacher and ask him or her to write to the exam boards and universities.

Case study

'I want students in my department who demonstrate that they are genuinely interested in my subject and in my department, and so if I have places left once the A level results are out, I will be happy to consider students who have narrowly missed their offers, rather than reject them and give the places to students who are applying through Clearing. Having said that, I have also been able to accept some excellent Clearing students, so I would not discourage Clearing applicants from having a go. But in order to convince me, they will need to act quickly and provide me with evidence – an updated personal statement perhaps, showing reading and work experience, or a reference from their work experience.'

An admissions tutor for business studies

What to do if you hold an offer and get the grades

If you previously received a conditional offer and your grades equal or exceed that offer, congratulations! You can relax and wait for the university that you accepted as your firm choice to send you joining instructions.

Clearing

Students who are not holding any offers when the examination results are published, or who have failed to achieve the grades that they need, are eligible for Clearing. The Clearing system operates by publishing all remaining university vacancies on the UCAS website and in the national newspapers. Students can then find appropriate courses and apply directly to the university. This time, you do not go through UCAS. UCAS will send you a **Clearing Passport** which, when you have been made a verbal offer that you wish to accept, you then send to UCAS to confirm the place. Bear in mind that Clearing places at the top universities are scarce, and so you will need to act very quickly.

If you have only narrowly missed the required grades (for example, the AAC grade case described below), it is important that you and your referee contact the university to put your case before you are rejected. Sample text for an email is shown below.

If this is unsuccessful, and you cannot find a suitable Clearing place, you may need to consider retaking your A levels and applying again.

To: r.race@melchester.ac.uk
From: Lucy Johnson

A level results

Dear Mr Race

UCAS no 08-123456-7

I have just received my A level results, which were:
Mathematics A, Physics A, Economics C.
I also have a B grade in AS Philosophy.

I hold a conditional offer from Melchester of ABB and I realise that my grades may not meet that offer. Nevertheless I am still determined to study economics and I hope you will be able to find a place for me this year.

My head teacher supports my application and is emailing you a reference. Should you wish to contact him, his details are: Mr C. Harrow, tel: 0123456 7891, fax: 0123 456 7892, email: c.harrow@melchester.sch.uk.

Yours sincerely

Lucy Johnson

■ Retaking your A levels

The grade requirements for retake candidates are often higher than for first timers. Most AS and some A2 units can be taken in January sittings, and some boards offer other sittings. This means that a January retake is often technically possible, although you should check carefully before taking up this option, since there may be complications because of, for example, coursework.

The timescale for your retake will depend on:

- the grades you obtained first time
- the syllabuses you studied.

If you simply need to improve one subject by one or two grades and can retake the exam on the same syllabus in January, then the short retake course is the logical option.

If, on the other hand, your grades were DDE and you took your exams through a board which has no mid-year retakes for the units that you require, you probably need to spend another year on your retakes. You would find it almost impossible to master syllabus changes in three subjects and achieve an increase of nine or ten grades within the 17 weeks that are available for teaching between September and January.

Independent sixth-form colleges provide specialist advice and teaching for students considering A level retakes. Interviews to discuss this are free and carry no obligation to enrol on a course, so it is worth taking the time to talk to their staff before you embark on A level retakes. Many FE colleges also offer (normally one-year) retake courses, and some schools will allow students to return to resit subjects, either as external examination candidates or by repeating a year.

07 Qualifications, training and careers

Many graduates pursuing a business or financial career have degrees in the subject but not all fall into this category. Some have studied another subject such as statistics, psychology or English and join a company on its graduate management-training programme. Others have completed vocational courses. It is also possible to become a successful businessperson by working your way up through the ranks from the shop floor – but this is much less common today than it was in the past.

Because managers and economists work in so many different businesses and organisations, and their roles vary from organisation to organisation, there is no single route to a career in these fields. However, you will need certain skills and talents, and a strong academic background will help. The following are academic qualifications that will open up opportunities and help you on your career path.

A levels and equivalent

Nearly all A level subjects are acceptable for business, economics and management degrees. A broad selection of subjects would prove a very good grounding for a business career. It is not necessary to take Business Studies or Economics at A level, but it's quite common for General Studies and Critical Thinking to be discounted by some universities. You will need to pay particular attention to each university's entrance requirements. Also note that a modern language A level could be an advantage if you apply for a job with an international company.

You will need to have good grades for the best higher education and employment opportunities. University admissions tutors and, subsequently, employers will look for good A level and AS level grades as part of their selection criteria. Specific grades will vary but the 'old' universities and the big organisations will certainly look for – and get – candidates with mostly grades A and B. A choice of AS level subjects demonstrating breadth, for example a social science, an arts subject, a language and a numerical subject is an advantage.

The degree

Studying a first degree in economics, business studies or management is not a requirement for a career within these disciplines. Many students will follow an unrelated degree course and then take professional qualifications afterwards. First degree courses generally give a broader base than can be gained by studying for a single professional qualification. They provide a foundation in the principles and techniques of modern finance, business and management and the directions in which they are developing. You will be trained in one or more specialist aspects of economics, business studies or management and will have contact with the real world. You will also learn about the sources and uses of information and methods of investigation.

As you will have seen from Chapter 1, there is considerable scope for overlap between subjects studied as part of economics, business studies or management degrees, and it is possible to steer your degree into the direction that you want to specialise in whilst at the same time learning about related topics. A degree in economics would normally include the opportunity to study modules on accounting and finance, banking, and management science. A management degree could also include these topics, but would also include some psychology, business studies and law. Unlike management or economics degrees, a business studies degree is not all taught by conventional lectures and seminars. It also involves extensive project-based work, case studies, business games and other simulations of the business world. So by the time you graduate you are as prepared as possible for work.

Sandwich courses are usually the more directly vocational courses and are more frequently offered by the 'new' universities. Nearly all the four-year courses include 12 months' practical training, i.e. in industry, gaining work experience. The practical training occupies either the whole of the third year – a 'thick' sandwich – or two or more periods of up to six months in different years – a 'thin' sandwich.

Many universities now arrange for placements to be spent working abroad and provide language tuition for students before they depart.

Case study

'The competition to get on to the scheme was intense and we all really had to jump through hoops to secure our places. This started with a fairly straightforward one-to-one interview with the graduate recruitment manager on my university campus. I had prepared well for the interview and had done my research on the company, including looking at their website, and I think this really helped and it certainly gave me confidence. I'd also had a mock interview at my careers service which was extremely useful. The next stage was an all-day event at the employer's premises. I was with about eight other candidates and we went through a combination of individual interviews with more senior staff and some group exercises, where they gave us a hypothetical problem and asked us as a group to discuss it and come up with some recommendations. I guess it didn't matter too much what our ideas were, as long as they made some sense, but I think what they were really looking for was to see how we interacted with each other. That included how we communicated our ideas, but also how we listened to others and took their ideas on board. We were also given a 30-minute numeracy test where we were not allowed to use a calculator – so remember to brush up on your tables! I must have passed all those tests as I was then offered a place on the scheme to start the following September.'

Graham, a graduate in mathematics and management, now a graduate trainee

Skills and qualities

A degree, even a very good one, is not enough to get on to a prestigious training scheme with a notable company. Graduate recruiters are not usually bothered about your particular degree subject – but they will often want their management trainees to be numerate. Subjects such as marketing, mathematics or statistics, economics, finance or business studies can give you an edge, but some employers still prefer the traditional academic subjects such as history or classics, even for marketing consumer products. However, there are no degree subjects that completely preclude a graduate from entry to a management training scheme.

If you have a good academic background, it will be your personal qualities that will often win you the job. Most companies' recruitment brochures will give you a fairly comprehensive list of skills and qualities they are looking for. Here are some of them:

- communication skills (these are paramount)
- the ability to think logically and clearly and to analyse accurately
- the ability to research facts and to be able to assess what information is important
- absorption of, assessment of the importance of and seeing the implications of lots of very detailed information
- organisational ability
- the ability to work with anyone at any level and get the best out of them
- building and maintaining working relationships, and summing up people accurately
- the ability to cooperate and contribute to a team
- numeracy
- self-confidence
- sound business awareness

- natural authority and leadership
- the ability to think strategically, see the whole picture and conceptualise
- the ability to keep targets in focus and make sure they are reached
- the ability to motivate others, recognise their potential and delegate responsibility
- high ethical standards
- the ability to prioritise information and tasks.

Career opportunities

Business and management

Graduates in business and management enter a very wide range of careers. These include accountancy, investment banking, insurance, management consultancy, information technology, marketing, business journalism, the media and the legal profession – to name but a few. The list of options is almost endless, but it must be highlighted that many of the careers and employers recruiting such graduates are increasingly global.

How often do you hear someone say *'I'd like to work in business'* or *'I'd like to be a manager'*? These are not uncommon career aims, but more often than not people do not have a real understanding of what being a business person or manager actually involves. The terms are sometimes used as meaning 'being successful' rather than anything to do with the concept of the work. So, first things first: if you are thinking about a career in business and management you need to find out what management means and what the typical functions or departments within businesses are.

Whenever you open a newspaper and look at the jobs section, every second advertisement has the word 'manager' in its title. Is this just a ploy to attract applicants or is it that some form of management is integral to many jobs? And if so, what do all these people do? Well, they all do different things, and work for an enormous variety of organisations. Yet at the same time they all have certain responsibilities and tasks in common.

The most straightforward definition of *management* in business terms could be 'the achievement of objectives through other people'. So, the primary difference between managerial and other types of work is that it involves getting other people to do the necessary work rather than doing all the tasks yourself.

Essentially, anyone who manages is responsible and accountable for making sure that whatever department or project they are in charge of runs smoothly and successfully. (Depending on the type of employer, this usually means profitably too!) Now this obviously means that you bask in the glory – and hopefully the profits – when all goes well. But when things go wrong, as they inevitably do at times, the manager is the person who will be taken to task because it is he or she who has the ultimate responsibility for what happens. So you can draw the following conclusions about the role of management in business.

■ Every job has some managerial aspects. Even the most junior clerical workers must ensure that others cooperate with them so that they can do their job.

■ No job is exclusively managerial. Everyone has to perform some tasks for themselves.

■ Management is not just about status or being paid better. Some professionals and other specialists, with no real management responsibilities, are often more senior and have a higher salary than many managers.

■ The term management also covers a vast range of other activities, including supervision, organisation, administration and leadership. (The job title 'executive' is sometimes used in the same context as 'manager'.)

Management is undoubtedly a skill in its own right and is essentially the same in whatever field it is carried out. Good managers are not confined to managing work which they are capable of doing themselves. Indeed, in the higher levels of management it can be an advantage not to have the bias that specialist knowledge can produce.

Beginning your career

A number of large companies have graduate training schemes for new graduates. With such companies, training is usually undertaken in house through formal programmes and on-the-job experience, and is sometimes combined with study for a professional qualification. However, lots of graduates start their careers in a small organisation which may not have any formal training programme. Although this is less structured, it is possible to get a wealth of early experience and responsibility by being thrown in at the deep end, while gaining an excellent overview of how the whole organisation operates.

There is no right or wrong answer regarding whether it is better to join a big or small organisation initially. You should consider how much structure and formal training you want and look for an organisation that will give you what you are looking for. If a firm belongs to the Investors in People government initiative, it will place great emphasis on training and career development. Traditionally, people reach a management position after a number of years of experience in a specialist function, such as sales, marketing, personnel or finance.

Many firms have moved away from the traditional hierarchical structure based on business functions (like production, marketing, etc.) to one based on project teams. Working in a smaller team like this can be very exciting, as there is often a greater sense of urgency and camaraderie amongst the various members. You need to learn how to reach decisions within a group and realise that everyone is different but that this does not mean they do not have important skills to contribute. You also learn that no one is perfect and everyone can make mistakes – including you!

Information technology (IT) really has changed the way we are able to work. Some firms now even consist of 'virtual teams', i.e. people who work together but do not share an office to do this. They may be scattered geographically and communicate via their mobile phones and the internet. They may only work for that company on a few days every week, doing something else for the rest of their time.

Typical business functions

We will now look at some of the most popular areas of business and management in more detail.

Marketing

The marketing function in business is to make people aware that a product or service exists, and encourage people to buy it. This often requires identifying the most likely groups of buyers and targeting them in specific ways. TV ads, for example, require considerable planning and market research. Marketing professionals will have researched the product and its rivals and identified how and where they want to place their product in the market in order to maximise sales, or promote brand loyalty, or achieve market penetration, etc. They will commission an advertising agency to come up with a suitable advertising campaign and monitor how advertising affects sales. Psychologists are often involved in devising advertising slogans or images that will stick in the mind and which will be recalled or will influence us when we see the product.

Careers in marketing are often varied; many people who have worked in marketing later move on to advertising agencies or to work as publicity consultants. Marketing tends to attract people who are creative and good at thinking up original and innovative ideas. However, there are also many jobs in market research that require people who can direct discussion groups, design and conduct surveys and process the statistical evidence. For these jobs it is important to have good numeracy and communication skills.

Most business studies degrees will include modules on marketing. If you are sure that you want a career in marketing, you could decide to choose a joint honours degree such as business studies with marketing, or single honours degree in marketing. Some art colleges will also offer specialised marketing degree courses, such as fashion marketing.

These tend to involve more creative and practical work than those offered on the more traditional courses.

In addition to the more general business and management degrees you might want to look at more specialised courses.

Case study

After graduating with a BA in Business Studies, Caroline started her career as a marketing assistant in the marketing department of a pharmaceutical company.

The team I worked with analysed markets worldwide to find which would be most suitable to promote our new products into. This gave me a lot of practical and wide-ranging experience. The company really believes in investing in staff and I was also sent on numerous training courses in all aspects of marketing techniques, so I had a good mixture of formal training and hands-on experience. After a few years, I decided that although I really loved the job in marketing, I came into contact a lot with the advertising industry – and that was a big attraction.

So Caroline decided to try to progress her career in this area.

I'd built up many valuable contacts through my marketing experiences, so talking to people I knew in the advertising industry helped me identify the sort of jobs I could go for, and the companies that had vacancies. Eventually I was successful – I've just been offered a job as an account executive with a major advertising agency!

Caroline, graduate with a BA in Business Studies

Sales

Another aspect of business is sales. This work is increasingly commission only. In other words, if you do not sell anything you do not get paid. On the other hand, if you are good at selling, the rewards can be fantastic.

What you sell will depend on the business you work in. Books, advertising, professional services, time-shares, cars, stocks and shares, ideas, computer software – anything that a business produces needs to be sold. The work may involve travelling as a rep or may be desk-based telesales, for example. As a manager you will also be responsible for the sales team, whether it is in house or made up of reps based around the country or abroad.

You can be taught sales techniques as part of a business studies course, but you need a basic aptitude to sell really effectively. If you have natural selling skills, this might be an area to consider. If you are not sure whether a job in sales is for you, your summer vacations could be a useful testing period. There are lots of jobs where you could try out your sales technique!

As well as being an integral part of a business-related degree, there are more specialised degree courses available that focus on this area, such as marketing and sales or sales management.

Case study

Neil has been working at a large retail outlet as a Department Manager for the past two years. He graduated three years ago with a 2.i degree in business studies from Kingston University and successfully got his job by applying through the university milk round. After taking a year off, which combined temporary work with travelling, he joined the company on its 18-month graduate training programme. Neil says:

My training has been excellent and I am still learning all the time. I have been on short courses covering topics such as teamwork, negotiating skills, customer service, and management skills. I started my training in the soft furnishings department and am now the Department Manager for the books department. I have been exposed to all aspects of running a department, from working on the shop floor, serving customers, to learning about stocktaking and display.

Each day is totally different – you never know what to expect when dealing with customers. Most are very nice but you do have to be tactful when dealing with tricky situations. You need plenty of stamina and flexibility but the rewards are well worth the hard work when you see the sales figures boosted. And the satisfaction of working with your team is tremendous.

Neil, department manager of a large retail outlet

Personnel

Personnel work, or **human resources (HR)**, as it is often called, covers every aspect of a business to do with the people in it. As a personnel officer you would be involved in the recruitment and training of staff, implementing company policies and government legislation affecting employees, and maintaining employee records. In large companies human resources departments analyse staffing requirements, agree targets and devise selection procedures. They organise staff appraisals and administer training and management development policies, and deal with disciplinary matters as they arise. Personnel departments in some very large organisations will often be split into different functions, such as training and graduate recruitment.

In smaller companies there may only be one or two people who have to cover all personnel issues, and these may be a small part of their whole job function. So if you were to join a small administrative department you might get more of an overview of personnel than in quite a large company, where your training may be more specialised. In small companies, it is also quite common that departmental managers deal with personnel issues such as training and discipline.

Personnel work is often challenging and emotionally demanding. The skills required include objectivity (the ability to see all sides of a problem), a reasonable level of numeracy, organising skills and an understanding of all types of people.

Management degrees are particularly suitable for students who are interested in following this route, because they will include modules on the psychology of dealing with people. There are also legal issues to be taken into consideration – these are also likely to be offered as part of a management-related degree. Most business courses will also provide students with the opportunity to find out more about personnel work and HR, but it is likely to form a smaller part of the course. You might also look at business and personnel, or business and human resources management courses.

Case study

Alex graduated with a 2.i degree in business studies. In his final year he took human resources management as one of his major options, having decided he wished to pursue his future career in this area. Despite fierce competition he was successful in being offered a place on a graduate personnel training scheme with a major accountancy firm, which he has recently started.

Alex is convinced that his one year's industrial placement with a bank helped his credibility here. So far, his training has given him a thorough understanding of the firm, and he is now beginning to get involved in some recruitment and selection activities, as well as arranging presentations at various universities. He will shortly be starting the professional qualification for the Chartered Institute of Personnel and Development, which his employer will sponsor. Alex says:

I know it will be hard work to combine the demands of work with study, but I'm convinced it will be worthwhile and I'm really looking forward to it.

Alex, on a graduate personnel training scheme

Finance

The financial aspects of a business are commonly regarded as the most important. If there is no cash in the tills and the bank wants the overdraft repaid yesterday – that is trouble. All firms have accounts departments responsible for sending out invoices and chasing debtors, paying suppliers and generally drawing up the company's annual accounts. This is known as financial accounting and is concerned with keeping track of the financial side of the business after the transactions have happened. Financial accounting lets the senior management know how well the business has done in the past year. However, it does not prepare for the future. Planning for the future is called management accounting. Here firms draw up very extensive and detailed budgets for every department so that they can keep a tight control on costs and are therefore less likely to make mistakes in the year ahead. Both types of accounting make extensive use of IT.

Accountancy does not have to be boring and desk bound. It can be a good way to join a creative team in the media industry or film industry – areas that are often difficult to get into otherwise.

The financial sector covers a wide range of careers and employers. These include banks, building societies, insurance companies and accountancy firms. All of these organisations would be open to recruiting graduates with a degree in business and management, as long as their A level grades (or equivalent) are good enough and they have a good degree, which usually means a minimum 2.i.

For example, all the major clearing banks run graduate training schemes which would give you the opportunity to train and work in many aspects of the bank's function over a period of often around 18 months. This will usually mean moving around the country for your various placements. In the case of the banks, you will normally be encouraged to study for the Institute of Bankers' professional examinations. Once experienced, you may be promoted to, for example, a branch manager. In this role you may be involved with individuals and with corporate clients. As a trainee you might have a spell in a department marketing corporate services and then move into a role as a personal accounts executive.

In addition to their general graduate training schemes, most of the large banks also recruit graduates directly into their computing departments. This does not necessarily require you to have a computer science degree, and most of these training schemes are open to graduates from any degree discipline.

Most careers within the financial sector will require you to be meticulously accurate and be good with figures. You will also need to have good interpersonal skills, excellent IT skills and be able to work effectively as part of a team.

Business studies, economics and management degrees will all cover aspects of finance and accounting, as these are equally applicable to the running of a small business, a government organisation, or a country's economy. A business- or management-related degree will look at the more practical aspects of finance – accounting procedures, financial management, legal issues and banking procedures – whereas an economics degree will look at this on a larger scale and in a more mathematical and theoretical way.

There are also more specialised degrees available for those students who have a clear idea of their future directions: accounting, accounting and finance or banking and finance courses are widely available and very popular.

Purchasing

Most organisations, including manufacturing and insurance companies, as well as public-sector organisations, require expert purchasers or buyers. For example, each year the National Health Service spends in excess of £4 billion on drugs and sophisticated electronics. And central and local government spend well over £150 billion on supplies.

'Purchasing' is a term mainly used in industry. 'Buying' tends to be used in retailing, and other organisations will often use the term 'supplies'. But the principles of the job are the same. Purchasing managers are now part of a wider profession known as supply chain management. Purchasing is probably at its most complicated in the manufacturing industry, where products such as cars are assembled from many different components. The purchasing manager may be involved from the start, when the design engineers begin to specify the raw materials and the parts needed, starting to pinpoint suppliers and sorting out any problems on new designs.

Skills required for purchasing include the ability to work well with figures, accuracy and the ability to digest technical and other data quickly and easily, as well as excellent communication skills.

Business and management degrees will cover topics which are relevant to students interested in this area, and are likely to use case histories and current businesses as illustrations. Economics degrees will include courses in microeconomics (which deals with how individuals and businesses manage and plan their finances) and macroeconomics (how countries' economies depend on income and expenditure). These courses will treat purchasing in a more theoretical and mathematical way. You could also investigate purchasing and supply, or business and purchasing degree courses.

Transport management

Transport managers are responsible for the safety and efficiency of passenger or freight services. This might include managing and administering on a day-to-day basis at places such as airports, railway stations, ports and bus or freight depots. Tasks would include scheduling and timetabling. The role of the transport manager would also cover the commercial roles open to all businesses, like finance, marketing and personnel management.

If there is an accident, it is the job of the transport manager to investigate and take any necessary action. A vital task is to ensure that health and safety regulations are enforced.

To be successful in transport management you must be good at organising and planning and enjoy working with figures. It is important that you can remain calm under pressure, but are able to think quickly and logically on your feet. Teamwork and good interpersonal skills are essential.

Both business- and management-related degrees would provide the necessary knowledge and skills for a career in transport management. Some of the world's biggest businesses are involved in the movement of people and goods. You could also look at more specialised transport management degrees.

Project management

Many firms organise their staff into specific projects instead of according to the traditional functions of marketing, finance, personnel, etc. People who work on a specific project will come from a variety of different business backgrounds and be together for the duration of that project. They often work as a team, sharing tasks and responsibility, and are more focused on that one project.

Leading a project as project manager requires great skill but can also be very exhilarating.

Management degrees would be the most suitable for a student who is aiming at project management as a future career. There are many specialised degree courses available including building project management, project engineering and even public art project management.

Management consultancy

The Institute of Management Consultancy (www.imc.co.uk) defines a management consultant as an independent and qualified person who provides a professional service to business, the public and other undertakings.

Management consultants identify and investigate problems within a company concerned with strategy, policy, markets, organisation, procedures and methods. Generally a team is sent to spend time within the organisation to find out what the problems are. They then come up with a set of recommendations for action by collecting and analysing the facts, still keeping in mind the broader management and business implications. Finally, they discuss and agree on the most appropriate course of action with the client, and may remain within the company for a short period to help the client implement these strategies.

Management consultants are high fliers – they can be recruited from among top graduates, but they are usually people with business experience. The reason is that if you are going to have any credibility in advising others how to run their businesses, you need real-life understanding of such issues. You will also need to be quite sensitive and tactful and have a good deal of maturity. Excellent numeracy, teamwork and interpersonal skills are all essential, as is a strong academic background (usually meaning at least a 2.i degree from a prestigious university).

Management degrees would provide a good deal of useful background and training for anyone interested in a career in management consultancy. Given the need for analytical and numeracy skills, economics graduates would also satisfy this requirement. There are many very specialised management degrees on offer, which can be found using the 'Course Search' facility on the UCAS website.

Case study

Paula joined one of the leading strategy management consulting firms two years ago, following a BSc in Business Administration. Paula says:

> I chose management consultancy for a number of reasons. The training in business was rigorous and I had to be prepared to work extremely hard. It also gave me the opportunity to meet clients from a huge variety of sectors, which will give me the chance, if I want it later on, to move into industry, having gained an excellent background.

> My first project lasted six months, and I worked closely with three colleagues. I was regularly commuting to the north of England to help analyse and assess why a particular manufacturing company had been consistently dropping profits over a two-year period. After much research it was the job of the team to feed back our findings with a list of recommendations.

> From the beginning I had to get used to presenting my work to colleagues and then to our clients in a clear, logical and persuasive manner. At times, the pressure can be enormous for short periods of time. On average I work 55 hours per week. I have had two short-term overseas projects, one in France and one in Hong Kong. You are really rewarded for the actual work you do and that is a strong motivating factor for me. I can't think of a job I'd rather do!

> **Paula, a management consultant**

Large companies – general management

Large companies will often have general managers who are responsible for the general running and operational details of a business. Their role is to liaise with other departments, monitor how members of staff are recruited and make sure that training is kept up to date. The general manager is also responsible for ensuring that profit targets are met, as well as keeping an eye on the marketing and promotional aims of the organisation.

Several large businesses run training schemes for both school-leavers and graduates as management trainees. Most schemes give an initial period of training, often 12–18 months, where you receive placements in a number of departments within the organisation, such as finance, sales and marketing. This is a great opportunity to try out different areas and find out what you like and what you are good at – a bit like a Foundation course. At the end of the training period you can decide where you want to specialise.

A number of companies have fast-track management programmes with accelerated training and early responsibility. Many university management departments will also have close links with large companies in order to provide internships or training.

Small businesses

Large company management training schemes, especially with 'blue-chip' organisations, are always going to be the most competitive to get into. You will certainly get a good and thorough structured training from them, but you should not overlook the often excellent experience you can gain from a smaller organisation.

You will probably be thrown in at the deep end and you are unlikely to have very specific responsibilities, but you will see at close hand the prizes and pitfalls of a career in business. You will see demonstrated the differences effective marketing makes, and will gain first-hand experience of things like dealing with banks and coping with disgruntled customers – in other words, the reality of working in business.

Managing a small business requires practical skills as well as an understanding of theory. Most business degrees will focus on these skills.

Entrepreneurs

If you have got a good idea, have some experience of constructing cash-flow forecasts, and do not fear failure or hard work, setting up your own business could be your route into the world of business. Richard Branson started his empire while still at school, as did Alan

Sugar. You could also use Anita Roddick and Terence Conran as your role models, both of whom started international companies from small businesses.

It is more common for someone to set up on their own after gaining their experience in another organisation. If you are thinking of starting your own business, you will need a lot of the skills and business awareness that you can best gain from employment. Added to which, you will need to be innovative and creative, energetic and resilient. You will need to be persistent and prepared to work long hours. You will need to be realistic in your business plans, and able to adapt rapidly to changing circumstances. It can be very fulfilling to be self-employed, but make sure it is for you before choosing this route.

Successful entrepreneurs tend to be dynamic people with a clear vision of what they want to achieve. Degree courses cannot teach students to be successful entrepreneurs, but a degree in business studies will give a budding entrepreneur the practical skills and knowledge base to supplement his or her ambitions and ideas. There are many degree courses that focus on entrepreneurship, often combined with other disciplines such as mathematics or a language.

What makes a good manager?

Many students are attracted by the thought of a managerial career. It has the advantage of being open to any discipline and work is rewarded on merit – your worth is judged by your performance. A managerial career is not dependent on seniority, and it can offer its own rewards, stemming from practical achievement in a job where results can be measured. Whilst a degree in management will not automatically make you a good manager (nor would a business studies degree make you a successful businessperson), it does provide you with the academic and practical skills that are necessary for a successful career in management. But bear in mind that there are other ways to acquire these skills.

Different managerial roles require different skills, but a general idea of what companies require of their managers is given below.

Management skills

Managers today have to work in an ever-changing and complex business environment; they need to use an increasing number of analytical methods and techniques. An important skill lies in knowing which techniques to use in a given situation, and how to use them correctly. Here are the main skills you will need to be an effective manager.

Leadership

Good managers are also leaders. The real challenge of management lies in empowering your team to take charge of a project or goal and together achieve more than they believed they could possibly handle. On a management degree course, you would look at different leadership models.

Delegating

Management involves delegating power and responsibility appropriately, not preventing others from developing by hanging on to everything, but not giving unachievable workloads or having impossible expectations.

Getting things done

Good managers are the people who get things done, and they do this by inspiring and encouraging the people working with them.

Teamwork

Teamwork plays a huge part in successful management and is the main reason why employers frequently ask candidates about their extracurricular achievements and activities. Playing a sport, taking part in dramatic productions or being involved in a school magazine or university society all show ability to work in a team.

Managing your own work

It is essential that the good manager is effective at managing their own workload well and setting standards for their team. This means setting an example in areas such as good organisation, timekeeping, commitment, personal presentation and honesty.

Managing stress

Because of the pressures of management, good managers will do whatever they can to avoid the effects of undue stress on their physical and mental health – and therefore their productivity. This means having problem-solving skills: noticing if a stressful situation is developing and affecting a team or its members, and being able to deal with it successfully.

Political awareness

Every organisation has its own culture and politics. Good managers will be aware of the context in which they work, including the sensitivities of other people and other departments, so that they can be most effective at motivating their teams.

Managing functions

The management role is broad ranging and responsibilities can be spread over several business areas or functions. For example:

- operations – maintaining and improving the delivery of whatever service or product for which they are responsible
- finance – budgeting and monitoring the use of the resources

- people – motivating those they work with
- information – communicating effectively with everyone at all levels.

Languages

Language skills are essential and already more than half of the world's population speaks a second language. It is vital to have a thorough understanding of the language and culture of a country. To enable effective communication with others you need to cope with the nuances of speech as well as understanding documents such as letters and reports. If you are an English speaker you can get by in Scandinavia, the Netherlands, Germany, much of Central and Eastern Europe and sometimes in France and Belgium without local language skills. (This would not, perhaps, be so easy in Spain or Italy.) But in any situation, you will always be at an advantage if you are able to hold at least a simple conversation in the language of the country you are working in.

Economics

Many economics graduates follow business or management careers. Economics degrees provide graduates with a range of analytical skills, and an in-depth knowledge of how domestic and global money markets operate. Businesses, in particular, that operate on a global scale, are keen to recruit economists. There are many other opportunities open to economics graduates. Economists are employed by banks and other financial institutions, public bodies, political parties, governments, NGOs and universities. Newspapers often undertake surveys to compile lists of the UK's top companies or biggest employers, and the majority of these will employ economists. Some of these will be banks, accountancy firms, or management consultants; but government bodies such as the NHS recruits economists. The government's own economic service employs over 1,000 economists.

Good economists are able to analyse information, mostly in numerical form, and to draw conclusions from it. They are generally strong mathematicians as well as being able to understand theoretical models and apply them to real-life situations.

Case study

Jenny studied A levels in Economics, Mathematics and Physics at a sixth-form college in London. She found all three subjects worked well together, and she was able to use ideas and techniques from her physics to help her with her economics.

I found that being able to understand the ideas behind proving theories and equations in A level Physics to be very helpful in my economics. In physics, you look at experimental results and then see how they can either prove, disprove or modify an equation or theory. A good example of this is in quantum physics, where one set of experiments seems to prove that light is a wave, whereas another set shows it is a particle – two very different things. Economics is the same, but the experiments are on a much larger scale – the global economy, for example! Economists come up with conflicting models to try to explain or predict how economies can develop and change, and we then try to see whether the results of the 'experiment', that is, what is actually happening in the world, support the theories.

At university, Jenny chose an economics degree course that involved a good deal of mathematical applications, as she enjoyed this aspect of the subject. She now works for a large international bank, looking at the impact of changes in commodity prices and how they affect the economy.

Jenny, employed by a large international bank

08 Current issues

The recent turbulence in the global financial markets demonstrates the unpredictability of the world of business and finance. Most people would not have guessed that some mortgage companies in the United States who lent money to people with very low incomes would have been the trigger for the collapse of banks and plummeting share prices across the world. Fluctuating oil prices, based on a range of factors, including political unrest and terrorism, have had an enormous impact on people's lives. Things move very fast in the financial and business worlds: demands change, companies grow and collapse, political issues affect prices and markets.

By the time you read this, many of the issues that made the headlines at the time of writing this book will no longer be relevant, and there will be new topics that I could not have guessed would be making the front pages. Above all, your knowledge of business, economics and management issues needs to be current and up to date. In this chapter, I have included a brief summary of some of the areas that you need to be familiar with. But beware: this is not a comprehensive list, and some of the topics may not be relevant by the time you are applying for your university courses. You must ensure that you prepare properly for your application by reading the quality newspapers on a daily basis, using websites such as www.bbc.co.uk to find out what is happening in your particular field of interest, reading magazines such as *The Economist*, and watching the news on television.

The credit crunch

The 'credit crunch' started with problems in the US housing market. A rise in interest rates caused many people to default on their mortgages, because the mortgage companies had lent them more money than they could afford to pay back. The term 'sub-prime mortgages' describes mortgages given to people with very low incomes. The mortgage companies often sold the debts to banks, and so the problem began to escalate. We began to read about the 'credit crunch' – a shortage of money available to be lent from banks to banks, or from banks to the public. Some banks collapsed because they ran out of money. When banks collapse, the markets and the public lose confidence because savings are at risk, and this has an effect on share prices. The BBC website contains a very detailed and clear timeline showing how the problems began, and how they developed and escalated.

▮ Oil prices

Oil prices more than doubled between January 2007 and January 2008, spiked again in the summer of 2008 and they continue to fluctuate dramatically. When the price of oil rises, it affects airlines, businesses, households and the cost of goods. The 2007 price rises started because of political problems in some oil-producing countries, such as Nigeria; and because of the risk of instability in the Middle East due to political violence in Pakistan. At the same time, the world's demand for oil was increasing rapidly because of the dynamic economic growth of China and India. The supply of oil is controlled by a cartel of oil-producing countries, OPEC, which decides how many barrels of oil can be sold each month, in order to ensure that its members get the best possible rewards from their resources.

▮ Environmental issues

Rising oil prices, diminishing stocks of fossil fuels and, above all, global warming have changed the ways that businesses and governments operate. There is a growing awareness amongst consumers and politicians that changes have to be made, and that 'going green' is going to be more than just an altruistic aim. More and more businesses are now trying to market themselves as being more eco-friendly than their competitors, and governments are keen to show potential voters that they are doing the same. The picture, however, is not a simple one. As an example, take the global rise in food prices between summer 2007 and summer 2008. There were many reasons behind this, such as bad weather and rising transport costs, but it also happened because many farmers around the world were encouraged to grow bio-fuels rather than food in order to try to reduce the reliance on fossil fuels. It will be interesting to see whether the trend towards greener (often more expensive) products and policies continues in the face of a global economic downturn.

▮ Globalisation

When the UK joined the EU it was known as the 'Common Market' because it broke down barriers for trade between the member countries and imposed some uniformity on trading conditions throughout the member countries. Globalisation means that the marketplace has opened up to such an extent that it is very easy to include the entire world. Communication, transport, raising of finance, etc. have all become much easier and firms have adapted their business strategies accordingly to improve the way they organise their business. Over half of all the international trade in the world is from one part of a multinational to another in a different country.

The standard wage in China is still under US$20 per week and firms obviously find it worth their while to build state-of-the-art factories there and ship the goods to their markets in Europe or the US. At first it was only manufacturing jobs that transferred to the Far East – but more recently, India in particular has become a nucleus for service industry jobs like call centres and computer programming. It is obviously impossible for the West to be able to compete against these wage levels and so it has to make the most of those aspects of the business where it still has a competitive advantage – in particular, new business ideas.

Businesses in Europe and the US are developing better and ever more efficient ways of managing their brands. 'Think global, act local' is a slogan that is often used here to mean that, despite globalisation, different cultures are still more different than we might think. Unless you have a truly international brand like McDonald's or Coca-Cola, your product may need to be slightly modified for each country.

The West also still has an advantage in technology and innovation, but it is not always easy persuading people to continue paying for this **intellectual property**. The fact that we can download many Open Source software programs from the internet means that many people no longer pay the licence fee to Microsoft. MP3 enables people to listen to music without paying royalties to the musicians.

◾ The impact of terrorism

The international threat of terrorism is having an impact on the global economy, but some sectors are feeling the impact more than others. Travel and tour companies have taken the biggest battering to date, due, in the short term, to the psychological impact on consumers who are afraid to fly or visit tourist locations in some parts of the world. Stores that have had major outlets in travel hubs such as airports and train stations have also suffered. WHSmith, for example, has seen a fall in share prices and is worried about the effect this will have on trade. Supermarkets, on the other hand are still trading comfortably, as people are feeling safer closer to home and are not neglecting their general routine in the light of heightened terror alerts.

Terrorism can have both a direct and indirect bearing on the economy. Terrorism impacts directly on the economy in the short term when it concerns the damage done to people's lives and property, immediate responses to the emergency, and rebuilding the affected systems, buildings and infrastructure. These costs, however, tend to be in proportion to the scale of the attack sustained. The indirect costs of terrorism mean that investors and consumers lose their confidence in the economy. Often strong consumer confidence goes a long way towards boosting an economy, a particular example being the US prior to the 2001 terror attacks, and how the economy is suffering as this confidence wanes. The threat of terrorism can also potentially affect productivity negatively, in the sense that transaction costs may be increased by higher insurance premiums and counter-terrorism regulations. The impact that terrorism will have on the global economy is being continually assessed and its full impact will depend on how long the campaign against terrorism continues and how quickly consumer confidence can be regained.

■ EU enlargement

May Day 2004 brought about the largest expansion of the European Union in its history: the 15 existing member states were joined by eight former Soviet-bloc countries and two Mediterranean islands, bringing the total membership to 25 countries. The ten new members (Czech Republic, Cyprus, Estonia, Hungary, Latvia, Lithuania, Malta, Poland, Slovakia and Slovenia) became equal members. The sixth stage of enlargement was finalised in January 2007 with the entry of Bulgaria and Romania.

The Balkan countries have been promised entry when they meet the economic conditions, and Croatia, Macedonia and Turkey have already been given **candidate status**. EU treaties, however, will have to be revised before any more countries can join as the Treaty of Nice stipulated that 27 members would be the maximum. Experts say the EU may be prepared to 'tinker' with treaties to allow Croatia in, but major reform will be necessary after that.

Joining the European Union does not immediately guarantee economic convergence and it will take some time before per capita GDP of the new member states matches that of the original 15. The new arrivals will have to rely on the other benefits of EU membership. The principal benefits of entry into the European Union, beyond political stability and economic openness, are not the regional aid they receive but the liberal movements of goods, capital and labour.

Goods and capital can move freely, but the free movement of labour has met with some opposition initially. Some in the West object to the influx of masses from the East, while some in the East are unhappy about losing their best academics and professionals to the West. Restrictions can potentially be placed on workers from Bulgaria and Romania but cannot be continued for more than seven years. Countries that impose restrictions must inform the European Commission why they think the foreign workers would distort their labour market. It is not difficult to understand why the new members will seem attractive to investors and importers, with their cheap labour costs and lower taxes. The benefits may be short lived, however, as these aspects will undoubtedly change with further integration.

Growth of China

Businesses have become increasingly international in the last decade and the world has become a smaller place in which to trade. The three regional trading areas – Europe, the Americas and Asia – are all competing for dominance, and the dominant partnerships are ever changing. China has proved that it can live up to its potential to perform on the world economic stage: its economy has experienced an incredible boom since the 1990s and has regularly been showing double-digit percentage growth since then. China became a member of the World Trade Organization in 2001 and is currently working on building the instruments and mechanisms needed to float the renminbi currency on the foreign exchange markets. Businesses in the West have had to make radical changes to their structures, systems and working measures to compete with the lower labour costs and flexible manufacturing systems in Asia, and will need to continue this review to stay competitive in the global marketplace.

The 2008 Beijing Olympic Games raised the country's profile internationally and provided China with an unprecedented shop window for the rest of the world, resulting in increased trade.

The recent global economic downturn, although precipitated by the credit problems that affected European and American banks and mortgage lenders, has had an effect on China, because China's growth is based on exports. In the first half of 2008, China's exports grew by 22% compared to the same period the previous year. But the growth for the same period in 2007 compared to 2006 was nearly 26%, indicating a slowing down of the growth of the economy. Added to this, imports were up by 30%, resulting in a $10 billion reduction in China's trade surplus. Every 1% decline in the US GDP is estimated to cause a 4% drop in China's growth of exports.

Costs are also rising in China as the workforce becomes more aware of its earning potential, and as the cost of imported raw materials and fuel rises. China is also, as a result of pressure from the West, spending more money on protecting the environment.

Business case histories

Morgan Spurlock's documentary *Super Size Me* had a huge impact on the image of McDonald's and could be said to have influenced the significant changes that McDonald's have recently made to their menus. Spurlock's experiment consisted of him eating McDonald's meals for breakfast, lunch and dinner every day for 30 days, trying everything on the menu as he did so. At the same time, he minimised the amount of physical exercise he was doing in order to emulate the average American. His audiences were appalled by what they were seeing – witnessing at first hand his body's reactions to this experiment. McDonald's then made some important announcements about changes to their menus. The first to be made was that super-sizing (massive portions of fries and Coke) was to be abolished and that the 'Happy Meal' would become the 'Go Active Happy Meal', complete with salad, free exercise manual and step-ometer.

The above example shows how an unexpected or unanticipated event can have a significant impact in the business world. If you are applying to study a business or management subject, you should have some examples at your fingertips of how (and why) companies and businesses grow, decline, change, adapt or develop. But don't simply do your research, close your file and forget about it until your interview. Things change all the time, and so you need to be constantly updating your knowledge of the businesses or business areas that you have been looking at.

Here are some suggestions for your research. This is only a very small selection of the many fascinating areas of business that you could look at:

- changes in the airline industry due to oil price changes – large car-riers and budget airlines
- the decline and revival of famous brand names – Marks & Spencer is a good example
- mergers between financial institutions – the recent global financial crisis has changed the face of banking. You might want to look at how the UK government has begun to instigate the nationalisation of some banks
- the organic food industry
- how the large sportswear companies have acted in the face of pub-licity about the use of Asian 'sweat shops' that produce, very cheaply, their expensive clothes, shoes and sports equipment.

Business ethics

A growing number of companies are realising that they do have respon-sibilities beyond merely returning dividends to shareholders. The term 'stakeholder' is used to mean all the other people, organisations and the environment that the firm impacts on. Some firms are so concerned with the ethical impact of their products that they monitor all the stake-holders of their suppliers as well as how their product will eventually be disposed of. This is known as the 'cradle to grave' approach. 'Triple bot-tom line' is a term used to describe the economic, social and environ-mental performance of a company.

One business director was noted for saying: 'Every business has an impact on society. The choice is to manage it or not to manage it. And why would anyone choose not to manage it?' Brands have been marketed so successfully that they appear to have a very real personality. This means that consumers choose brands depending on what they feel about these brands, and brand management is all about keeping your brand's image reliable, cool or ethical in the minds of your consumers. This is not an easy task and firms will tend to spend large amounts on specialist qualitative research into the opinions of their market.

GlaxoSmithKline, Britain's third largest drug company, was very heavily criticised at the World Trade Organization conference at Seattle for pricing its anti-AIDS drugs so high that poorer countries could not afford them. In contrast, the GlaxoSmithKline African Malaria Partnership awards grants totalling over US$1.5 million for malaria research and aid, and hardly anyone knows about this. This shows that often the problem is as much one of public image as what the company actually does.

Ultimately, decisions within companies are taken by the people who manage that company. Sixty-two per cent of firms say that they are likely to be influenced to be more socially active by their own employees. Graduates tend to choose the company they want to work for, carefully based on their own perceptions of what that company believes in. This is particularly the case when the economy is on the upturn and there are plenty of jobs for new graduates to choose from.

Work–life balance

People are increasingly working more flexibly. They may have two or more part-time jobs or may work freelance on a variety of often overlapping projects. Some of this may be done from home, from a laptop abroad or in an office where people 'hot-desk' (just come in to use the facilities from any desk that is free). This means that the division between work and leisure is increasingly blurred.

Most EU countries have signed the Social Chapter of the Maastricht Treaty, which forbids firms to ask their employees to work more than 48 hours in any week. There is an increasing amount of medical evidence about the damaging effects of overwork. If you work a 60-hour week you will also tend to be less efficient and make mistakes that might be costly to rectify. In the UK, we tend to work much longer hours than our European counterparts.

Managing change

Perhaps the overriding theme within the business world today is the speed at which change is occurring. The Japanese coined the term 'kaizen' to mean 'continuous improvement': everything that you do can always be improved upon.

The fact that the firm's competitors are constantly improving themselves and that profit margins are getting tighter and tighter means that there is all the more pressure to improve yourself as well, otherwise you may go under.

There are whole areas of business management concerned solely with how this change should be implemented. Change can be disruptive and some employees may resist it.

Knowledge management

Knowledge management is concerned with the most efficient ways of making information available to everyone who needs to know things, giving each as much as they need without falling into information overload. There is nothing more tedious than a computer printout that tells you everything about every department so that you then have to spend hours extracting the information you actually wanted.

A highly competitive firm should know what resources it has amongst its staff so that is it able to use these to their optimum. For example, they may have a native Spanish speaker whose talents could be invaluable in a certain transaction.

Further information

The UCAS tariff

Full details of the UCAS tariff points system can be found on the UCAS website. For A levels and AS levels, the tariff point system is shown below.

Table 6 The UCAS tariff system

AS grade	Tariff points	A level grade	Tariff points
A	60	A	120
B	50	B	100
C	40	C	80
D	30	D	60
E	20	E	40

So, a university might ask for 300 points, and the offer might specify that this is applies to the three A level subjects. To satisfy the offer, the student would need to achieve either ABC, AAD, or BBB. If the offer allows the student to include the fourth AS subject, then some of the combinations that would be acceptable are shown below.

Table 7 Combinations of grades that total 300 points

A level	AS level
BBC	E
BCC	C
CCC	A

If you receive a 'points' offer from a university, you should ensure that you are clear whether it includes just the A level grades, the A level and AS grades, or whether other qualifications that have a UCAS tariff (such as Key Skills or certain music examinations) can be included as well.

Other qualifications and the tariff point system

Table 8 International Baccalaureate tariff points

Grade	Tariff points
45	768
44	744

Grade	Tariff points
43	722
42	698
41	675
40	652
39	628
38	605
37	582
36	559
35	535
34	512
33	489
32	466
31	442
30	419
29	396
28	373
27	350
26	326
25	303
24	280

Table 9 Irish Leaving Certificate tariff points

Grade		Tariff points
Higher	Ordinary	
A1		90
A2		77
B1		71
B2		64
B3		58
C1		52
C2		45
C3	A1	39
D1		33
D2	A2	26
D3	B1	20
	B2	14
	B3	7

Table 10 Scottish Highers tariff points

Grade					Tariff points
Advanced Higher	Higher	Intermediate 2	Standard Grade	Core Skills	
A					120
B					100
C					80
D	A				72
	B				60
	C				48
	D	A			42
			Band 1		38
		B			35
		C	Band 2		28
				Higher	20
				Intermediate	10

Useful addresses

Association of Chartered Certified Accountants (ACCA)
29 Lincoln's Inn Fields
London WC2A 3EE
020 7059 5000
www.acca.org.uk

British Chambers of Commerce
65 Petty France
London SW1H 9EU
020 7654 5800
www.chamberonline.co.uk

Chartered Institute of Logistics and Transport
Earlstrees Court
Earlstrees Road
Corby NN17 4AX
01536 740100
www.ciltuk.org.uk

Chartered Institute of Management Accountants
26 Chapter Street
London SW1P 4NP
020 8849 2251
www.cimaglobal.com

Chartered Institute of Marketing
Moor Hall
Cookham

Maidenhead SL6 9QH
01628 427500
www.cim.co.uk

Chartered Institute of Personnel and Development
15 The Broadway
London SW19 1JQ
020 6612 6200
www.cipd.co.uk

Chartered Institute of Purchasing and Supply
Easton House
Church Street
Easton on the Hill
Stamford PE9 3NZ
01780 756777
www.cips.org

Chartered Management Institute
Head Office
Management House
Cottingham Road
Corby NN17 1TT
01536 204 222
www.managers.org.uk

Chartered Quality Institute
12 Grosvenor Crescent
London SW1X 7EE
020 7245 6722
www.thecqi.org

Confederation of British Industry
Centrepoint
103 New Oxford Street
London WC1A 1DU
020 7379 7400
www.cbi.org.uk

Development for Employment and Learning of Northern Ireland
Adelaide House
39-49 Adelaide Street
Belfast BT2 8FD
028 9025 7777
www.delni.gov.uk

Federation of Small Businesses
Sir Frank Whittle Way

Blackpool Business Park
Blackpool FY4 2FE
01253 336000
www.fsb.org.uk

Freight Transport Association
Hermes House
St John's Road
Tunbridge Wells TN4 9UZ
08717 112222
www.fta.co.uk

Higher Education Funding Council for England
External Relations Department
Northavon House
Coldharbour Lane
Bristol BS16 1QD
0117 931 7317
www.hefce.ac.uk

Higher Education Funding Council for Wales
Linden Court
Ilex Close
Llanishen
Cardiff CF14 5DZ
029 2076 1861
www.hefcw.ac.uk

Institute of Administrative Management
6 Graphite Square
Vauxhall Walk
London SE11 5EE
020 7091 2600
www.instam.org

Institute of Chartered Secretaries and Administrators
16 Park Crescent
London W1B 1AH
020 7580 4741
www.icsa.org.uk

Institute of Credit Management
The Water Mill
Station Road
South Luffenham
Oakham LE15 8NB
01780 722900
www.icm.org.uk

Institute of Directors
116 Pall Mall
London SW1Y 5ED
0207 839 1233
www.iod.com

International Institute of Management UK
Yr Efail
1 New Street
Kidwelly SA17 5D
www.iimau.com.au

Institute of Management Services
Brooke House
24 Dam Street
Lichfield WS13 6AB
01543 266909
www.ims-productivity.com

Management Consultancies Association
60 Trafalgar Square
London WC2N 5DS
020 7321 3990
www.mca.org.uk

Operational Research Society
Seymour House
12 Edward Street
Birmingham B1 2RX
0121 233 9300
www.orsoc.org.uk

The Packaging Society
The Institute of Materials, Minerals and Mining
1 Carlton House Terrace
London SW1Y 5DB
020 7451 7300
www.iom3.org

Prince's Trust
18 Park Square East
London NW1 4LH
020 7543 1234
www.princes-trust.org.uk

Scottish Funding Council
Donaldson House
97 Haymarket Terrace
Edinburgh EH12 5HD

0131 313 6500
www.sfc.ac.uk

Work Foundation
21 Palmer Street
London SW1H 0AD
020 7976 3500
www.theworkfoundation.com

Books

General higher education

Choosing Your Degree Course & University, Brian Heap, Trotman
Degree Course Offers, Brian Heap, Trotman
Getting into Oxford and Cambridge, Trotman
How to Complete Your UCAS Application, Trotman
Making the Most of University, Trotman
Mature Students' Directory, Trotman
Student Book, Trotman
Students' Money Matters, Gwenda Thomas, Trotman
The Ultimate University Ranking Guide, Trotman
University and College Entrance: The Official Guide, UCAS

Business, economics and management

Business Stripped Bare: Adventures of a Global Entrepreneur, Sir Richard Branson, Virgin Books
Business: The Ultimate Resource, produced by the Chartered Management Institute
Complete Small Business Guide, Colin Barrow, BBC Publications
Corporate Strategy, Igor Ansoff, Penguin
CRAC Degree Course Guides: Business and Economics, Trotman
The Credit Crunch: Housing Bubbles, Globalisation and the Worldwide Economic Crisis, Graham Turner, Pluto Press
Economics for Business and Management, Stuart Wall and Alan Griffiths
Effective Small Business Management, Norman M. Scarborough, Thomas W. Zimmerer and Doug Wilson
The Essential Drucker: The Best of Sixty Years of Peter Drucker's Essential Writing on Management, Peter Drucker, HarperCollins
Essential Manager's Manual, Robert Heller and Tim Hindle, Dorling Kindersley
Freakonomics: A Rogue Economist Explores the Hidden Side of Everything, Steven D. Levitt, and Stephen J. Dubner, Penguin
A Handbook of Management Techniques, M. Armstrong, Kogan Page
Human Resource Management: A Contemporary Approach, Tim Claydon and Julie Beardwell, Financial Times/Prentice Hall

Innovation and Entrepreneurship, Peter Drucker, Butterworth Heinemann

No Logo, Naomi Klein, Flamingo

Prospects series, Central Services Unit (CSU) Publications

The Shock Doctrine: The Rise of Disaster Capitalism, Naomi Klein, Penguin Books

The Snowball: Warren Buffett and the Business of Life, Alice Schroeder, Bloomsbury

The Real Deal: My Story from Brick Lane to the 'Dragons' Den', James Caan, Virgin Books

The Road Ahead: Level 3, Bill Gates, Penguin

Trotman's Green Guides: Business Courses, Trotman

The Undercover Economist, Tim Harford, Abacus

Understanding Organisations, Charles Handy, Penguin

What They Teach You at Harvard Business School: My Two Years Inside the Cauldron of Capitalism, Philip Delves Broughton

Which MBA?, George Bickerstaffe, Prentice Hall

■ Useful websites

Business and financial news
www.economist.com
www.ft.com
www.telegraph.co.uk/finance
www.businessweek.com
www.bbc.co.uk

Financial organisations
World Trade Organization www.wto.org
World Bank: www.worldbank.org

University entrance
www.ucas.com
http://education.guardian.co.uk/universityguide2009/